Standard Grade | General | Credit

History

General Level 2001

General Level 2002

General Level 2003

Credit Level 2001

Credit Level 2002

Credit Level 2003

© Scottish Qualifications Authority

All rights reserved. Copying prohibited. No part of this publication may be reproduced, stored in a retrieval system, or transmitted in any form or by any means, electronic, mechanical, photocopying, recording or otherwise.

First exam published in 2001.
Published by
Leckie & Leckie, 8 Whitehill Terrace, St. Andrews, Scotland KY16 8RN
tel: 01334 475656 fax: 01334 477392
enquiries@leckieandleckie.co.uk www.leckieandleckie.co.uk

Leckie & Leckie Project Team: Peter Dennis; John MacPherson; Bruce Ryan; Andrea Smith
ISBN 1-84372-102-3
A CIP Catalogue record for this book is available from the British Library.
Printed in Scotland by Scotprint.
Leckie & Leckie is a division of Granada Learning Limited, part of Granada plc.

Leckie✕Leckie
Scotland's leading educational publishers

Introduction

Dear Student,

This past paper book offers you the perfect opportunity to put into practice what you should know in order to do well in your exams. As these questions have actually appeared in the exam in previous years, you can be sure they reflect the kind of questions you will be asked this summer. Work carefully through the papers, not only to test your knowledge and understanding but also your ability to handle information and work through more thought-provoking questions. Use the answer booklet at the back of the book to check that you know exactly what the examiner is looking for to gain top marks. You will be able to focus on areas of weakness to sharpen your grasp of the subject and our top tips for revision and sitting the exam will also help to improve your performance on the day.

Remember, practice makes perfect! These past papers will show you what to expect in your exam, help to boost your confidence and feel ready to gain the grade you really want.

Good luck!

Acknowledgements

Leckie & Leckie is grateful to the copyright holders, as credited, for permission to use their material. Every effort has been made to trace the copyright holders and to obtain their permission for the use of copyright material. Leckie & Leckie will gladly receive information enabling them to rectify any error or omission in subsequent editions.

John Donald Publishers Ltd for an extract from *People and Society in Scotland, 1914–1990* by Tony Dickson and James H. Treble (2001 General paper p 7);

Canongate Educational for an extract copyright of Wendy Doran & Richard Dargie, and reproduced from *Changing Life in Scotland 1890–1980* (2002 General paper p 7);

The Bridgeman Art Library for a cartoon by James Gilray (2002 General paper p 9);

Mary Evans Picture Library for the photograph *Workers collecting their wages in washing basket* (2003 General paper p 21);

David King Collection for a photograph (2001 Credit paper p 19);

Pulse Publications for an extract from *Changing Life in Scotland and Britain* by Cameron, Henderson and Robertson (2002 Credit paper p 5);

Getty Images for a photograph (2002 Credit paper p 19).

The following companies/individuals have very generously given permission to reproduce their copyright material free of charge:
Pearson Education for:
an extract from *Living in Scotland* by A.D. Cameron (2001 General paper p 3);
an illustration and an extract from *Germany, 1919–1945: Modern Times Sourcebooks* by Maria McKay (2001 General paper p 23 and 2002 Credit paper p 20);
three extracts from *An Illustrated History of Modern Britain, 1783–1964* by D. Richards and J. Hunt (2002 General paper p 8 and 2002 Credit paper pp 8 & 9);
an extract from *Twentieth Century History* by Tony Howarth (2002 General paper p 10);
two extracts from *The American West 1840–1895* by R.A. Rees and S.J. Styles (2002 General paper p 15 and 2002 Credit paper p 15);
an extract from *Britain and Europe 1848–1980* by Martin Roberts (2002 General paper p 20);
an extract from *Germany 1815–1939* by F. McKichen (2002 General paper p 21);
an extract from *Waterloo to the Great Exhibition* by C. McNab and R. MacKenzie (2002 Credit paper p 2);
an extract from *Changing Lives: Scotland and Britain since 1830* by S. Wood (2002 Credit paper p 5);
an extract from *The World at Peace and War, 1890–1930* by Roy Wilsher (2002 Credit paper p 11);
an extract from *A History of the Twentieth Century* by Bryn O'Callaghan (2002 Credit paper p 13);
an extract from *The Penguin History of the United States of America* by Hugh Brogan (2002 Credit paper p 15);
an extract from *Russia in War and Revolution* by Josh Brooman (2002 Credit paper p 18);
an extract from *Lenin and the Russian Revolution* by Donald Mack (2002 Credit paper p 19);

G. C. Book publishers for an extract from *Reminiscences of Wigtonshire* by Samuel Robinson (2001 General paper p 5);

Modern Times: A History of Scotland, Book 5 by Alastair Gray (1989). Reproduced by permission of Oxford University Press (2002 General paper p 4);

Causeway Press for two extracts from *Britain Transformed* by Malcolm Falkus (2002 General paper p 4 and 2002 Credit paper p 4);

Her Majesty's Stationery Office for an extract from *The Scottish Railway Story* by Margaret Sanderson (2002 General paper p 5);

Imperial War Museum for two photographs (2002 General paper p 11 and 13);

An extract from *The Glasgow Herald*, 15th May 1941. Reproduced with the permission of The Herald (2002 General paper p 13);

Cambridge University Press for an extract from *The American West, 1840–1895* by Mike Mellor (2002 General paper p 14) and an extract from *Native Peoples of North America* by Susan Edmonds (2002 General paper p 15);

Spartacus Educational Publishers for two extracts from *Gandhi* by John Simkin (2002 General paper p 17 and 2002 Credit paper p 17);

Mary Evans Picture Library for a photograph (2003 General paper p21);

HarperCollins Publishers Ltd for an extract from *A History of the Scottish People* by T.C. Smout (1972) (2001 Credit paper p 3) and an extract from *Expansion, Trade and Industry* by C. Culpin (1993) (2002 Credit paper p 3);

Routledge for an extract from *A History of Scotland* by Rosalind Mitchison (2001 Credit paper p 2);

The Republican National Committee for a poster (2001 Credit paper p 14);

Punch Ltd for an illustration from *Gandhi* by Frederick William Rawding (2001 Credit paper p 16);

The Institute of Contemporary History and Wiener Library for a photograph (2001 Credit paper p 20) and a poster (2002 Credit paper p 21);

Causeway Press Ltd for an extract from *Britain Transformed* by Malcolm Falkus (2002 Credit paper p 4);

Penguin (UK) for an extract from *The Scottish Nation 1700-2000* by T.M. Devine (2002 Credit paper p 6);

The British Library for a photograph (2002 Credit paper p16);

Odhams Press for an extract from *As It Happened* by Clement Atlee (2002 Credit paper p 12);

The American Museum in Britain, Bath for the painting *Rocky Mountains – Emigrants Crossing the Plains* by Francis Palmer (2002 Credit paper p 14);

Pulse Publications for an extract from *Changing Life in Scotland and Britain* by Cameron, Henderson and Robertson (2003 Credit paper p 2).

2001 GENERAL

1540/402

NATIONAL QUALIFICATIONS 2001

WEDNESDAY, 30 MAY
G/C 9.00 AM – 10.30 AM
F/G 10.20 AM – 11.50 AM

HISTORY
STANDARD GRADE
General Level

Answer questions from Unit I **and** Unit II **and** Unit III.

Choose only **one** Context from each Unit and answer Sections A **and** B. The Contexts chosen should be those you have studied.

The Contexts in each Unit are:

Unit I— Changing Life in Scotland and Britain
    Context A: 1750s–1850s .... Pages 2–3
    Context B: 1830s–1930s .... Pages 4–5
    Context C: 1880s–Present Day .... Pages 6–7

Unit II— International Cooperation and Conflict
    Context A: 1790s–1820s .... Pages 8–9
    Context B: 1890s–1920s .... Pages 10–11
    Context C: 1930s–1960s .... Pages 12–13

Unit III— People and Power
    Context A: USA 1850–1880 .... Pages 14–16
    Context B: India 1917–1947 .... Pages 17–19
    Context C: Russia 1914–1941 .... Pages 20–21
    Context D: Germany 1918–1939 .... Pages 22–23

You must use the information in the sources, and your own knowledge, to answer the questions.

Number the questions as shown in the question paper.

Some sources have been adapted or translated.

UNIT I—CHANGING LIFE IN SCOTLAND AND BRITAIN

CONTEXT A: 1750s–1850s

SECTION A: KNOWLEDGE AND UNDERSTANDING

Study the information in the sources. You must also use your own knowledge in your answers.

Source A is a description of new farming methods.

Source A

> In Scotland the wind did not always blow when a farmer wanted it. So James Meikle invented a machine to winnow and thresh the grain whatever the weather might be. James Small invented a new plough with an iron blade. It could easily slice through the soil. It could be pulled by a pair of horses.

1. Explain in what ways the new farming inventions were better than the old methods. **4**

Source B was written by Dr John Snow in 1854 about an outbreak of disease in London.

Source B

> The most terrible outbreak of cholera has broken out in Broad Street. I suspect that the water in the much used pump in the street has been contaminated (polluted). In the last, large epidemic of 1848 almost 50 000 died from cholera.

2. How important was it to provide good water supplies in Britain in the nineteenth century? **3**

Marks

SECTION B: ENQUIRY SKILLS

The issue for investigating is:

> The population of Scotland rose between 1760 and 1820 as a result of improvements in food supply.

**Study the sources carefully and answer the questions which follow.
You should use your own knowledge where appropriate.**

Source C is from the autobiography of Thomas Somerville, a Scottish farmer. He wrote it in 1814.

Source C

> In the 1760s oat cakes formed the main food for my family. There was very little meat. Potatoes were still considered a luxury. The only vegetables grown were cabbages and turnips and they were of poor quality. People ate very little and very badly in my early life but now they eat much better. More babies are now born healthy and fewer die in their first months.

3. How useful is **Source C** for investigating causes of population growth in Scotland between 1760 and 1820?   **3**

Source D is from "Living in Scotland 1760–1820" by A. D. Cameron.

Source D

> The growth in population between 1750 and 1820 was caused by a rise in the birth rate. At this time of great economic change the demand for labour brought higher wages, earlier marriages and more births. There were also advances in hygiene and medical care.

4. What evidence in **Source C** agrees with the view that improvements in food supply caused a rise in the population?

    What evidence in **Source D** suggests that there were other reasons for population rise?   **5**

5. How far do you agree that the population of Scotland rose between 1750 and 1820 as a result of improvements in food supply?

    You must use evidence **from the sources** and **your own knowledge** to come to a conclusion.   **4**

[END OF CONTEXT IA]

Marks

UNIT I—CHANGING LIFE IN SCOTLAND AND BRITAIN

CONTEXT B: 1830s–1930s

SECTION A: KNOWLEDGE AND UNDERSTANDING

Study the information in the sources. You must also use your own knowledge in your answers.

Source A describes some railway improvements made between 1850 and 1914.

Source A

> By the late 19th century, main line express trains increased their average speed to over 60 mph. In 1895 there was serious competition between the two railway companies on the London to Aberdeen route. The fastest did the 524 mile journey in eight and a half hours. Improved locomotives made these new speeds possible. Heating was gradually introduced into passenger trains.

1. Explain in what ways travelling by train improved between 1850 and 1930. 4

Source B describes problems caused by a lack of clean water in the nineteenth century.

Source B

> Typhus, carried by lice from unwashed bodies, killed many people in the slums. Typhoid fever and cholera also resulted from dirty food or contaminated (polluted) water. The terrifying cholera epidemics, such as those of 1831–1832 and 1849, killed over 100 000 people.

2. How important for people's health was a clean water supply in the nineteenth century? 3

Marks

SECTION B: ENQUIRY SKILLS

The issue for investigating is:

> A better diet during the nineteenth century resulted in an increase in the population.

**Study the sources carefully and answer the questions which follow.
You should use your own knowledge where appropriate.**

Source C was written by Samuel Robinson in 1872. It gives his memories of life in South West Scotland.

Source C

> What an amazing change in eating habits have the years brought about. We now have a baker or two in almost every village. Almost everyone can afford to buy fresh butcher meat and more vegetables and sugar. This has produced a change in the health of the whole community. People now live longer and have larger families.

3. How useful is **Source C** for investigating causes of population growth in Scotland during the nineteenth century?   **3**

Source D is from "Nineteenth Century British History" by Michael Lynch, published in 1999.

Source D

> The main cause of the declining death rate was the drop in infant mortality (deaths). Children survived to become adults as a result of general improvement in the standard of people's health. Mothers were healthier and gave birth to healthier babies, more of whom survived.

4. What evidence in **Source C** supports the view that a better diet led to an increase in the population?

   What evidence in **Source D** reveals other reasons for an increase in the population?   **5**

5. How far do you agree that a better diet led to the growth of population in nineteenth century Scotland?

   You must use evidence **from the sources** and **your own knowledge** to come to a conclusion.   **4**

[END OF CONTEXT IB]

UNIT I—CHANGING LIFE IN SCOTLAND AND BRITAIN

CONTEXT C: 1880s–Present Day

SECTION A: KNOWLEDGE AND UNDERSTANDING

Study the information in the sources. You must also use your own knowledge in your answers.

Source A describes changes which motor transport has made to the countryside.

Source A

> Motor transport now takes villagers to the town. Children are collected by school bus. The town doctor's practice extends into the countryside. On the other hand, every beauty spot has been ruined by the need to build roads.

1. Explain in what ways motor transport affected the lives of people living in the countryside. **4**

Source B describes improvements to water supply.

Source B

> It was far better to stop disease from spreading by tackling their causes such as dirty water contaminated (polluted) by sewage. Water was cleaned up and by 1900 most towns had a clean supply. Proper sewage systems were built. Pipes and tunnels were laid to take waste to places where it was treated.

2. How important was clean water to the improvement of health in towns? **3**

Marks

SECTION B: ENQUIRY SKILLS

The issue for investigating is:

> A better diet has led to the growth of the population in Scottish towns.

Study the sources carefully and answer the questions which follow.
You should use your own knowledge where appropriate.

Source C is from a volume of the "Third Statistical Account of Scotland", written in 1960.

Source C

> The population of the main towns in Aberdeenshire has grown in the last 30 years. The town dwellers are better fed. They have more money to spend on food. They get more fruit when very small and also proper school meals and free milk. Most important of all, the milk has been cleaned up. Forty years ago it was common to find a sediment at the bottom of a glass of milk, but not now.

3. How useful is **Source C** for investigating the reasons for population growth in Scottish towns? 3

Source D is from "People and Society in Scotland, 1914–1990", published in 1992.

Source D

> During the period 1920–1960 more babies lived to the age of one and beyond. Fewer young adults died of tuberculosis. The major reason for this was the development of antibiotics. Less women died during childbirth and went on to have families.

4. What evidence is there in **Source C** that a better diet led to the growth of population?

   What evidence is there in **Source D** that other factors led to the growth of population? 5

5. How far do you agree that a better diet led to the growth of population in Scottish towns?

   You must use evidence **from the sources** and **your own knowledge** to come to a conclusion. 4

[END OF CONTEXT IC]

UNIT II—INTERNATIONAL COOPERATION AND CONFLICT

CONTEXT A: 1790s–1820s

SECTION A: KNOWLEDGE AND UNDERSTANDING

Study the information in the sources. You must also use your own knowledge in your answers.

Source A deals with the British Navy's attacks on the French fleet in 1798.

Source A

> Napoleon avoided Nelson and landed in Egypt where he defeated the Turkish army in the Battle of the Pyramids. Then Nelson, who had been sailing up and down the Mediterranean, destroyed the French fleet at the Battle of Aboukir Bay. Britain had gained naval control in the Mediterranean and occupied the island of Minorca.

1. How important was Nelson to Britain's victory in the war at sea? **3**

Source B describes some of the hardships faced by sailors during the Revolutionary Wars.

Source B

> The sailors' diet was badly balanced and this led to outbreaks of scurvy. This caused the sufferer's gums to swell, his teeth to fall out and swellings and sores to appear on his body. On the lower decks there was little fresh air, and the air was damp. The hammocks, often soaking, were jammed together. There were no washing facilities.

2. Describe conditions for British sailors serving on warships during the Revolutionary Wars. **4**

Marks

SECTION B: ENQUIRY SKILLS

The following sources are about the effect of war on French civilians.

**Study the sources carefully and answer the questions which follow.
You should use your own knowledge where appropriate.**

Source C describes problems facing France during the Revolutionary Wars.

Source C

> The French people were worried that the war was going against them. Another major concern was the high price of food. Prices were rising because, to pay for the war, the government was printing huge amounts of paper money. But the more bank notes were printed, the less they were worth. By 1793, angry French people found that a bank note was only worth half the amount printed on it.

3. According to the author of **Source C** what were the opinions of French people during the Revolutionary Wars? 3

Source D is from "European History 1789–1914" by C. A. Leeds.

Source D

> During the Revolutionary War France was in the midst of famine and lawlessness. Unemployment was high as industry had collapsed. Marat observed that the war was needed to "rid France of 300 000 armed criminals."

4. How fully does **Source D** describe the difficulties facing the French during the Revolutionary War?

   You should use **your own knowledge** and give reasons for your answer. 4

[END OF CONTEXT IIA]

UNIT II—INTERNATIONAL COOPERATION AND CONFLICT

CONTEXT B: 1890s–1920s

SECTION A: KNOWLEDGE AND UNDERSTANDING

Study the information in the sources. You must also use your own knowledge in your answers.

In **Source A** George Coppard describes his experiences of the First World War.

Source A

> The battalion moved up the communication trench to the front line trench at a snail's pace, suffering heavy casualties from shrapnel fire. We passed stretcher bearers with the many wounded and groups of tired troops going to the rear. We would soon be in the attack on the German front line.

1. What methods of fighting were used on the Western Front in the First World War? **4**

Source B is from a biography of Georges Clemenceau who represented France at the Treaty of Versailles.

Source B

> Clemenceau was a firm believer in the view that you must not negotiate with a German; you must dictate to him; on no other terms will a German respect you. Clemenceau was convinced that the negotiators at Versailles had to treat Germany firmly. He had twice seen his beloved France invaded by Germans in his lifetime. He was determined it must never happen again.

2. How important were Clemenceau's views on how Germany should be treated after the First World War? **3**

Marks

SECTION B: ENQUIRY SKILLS

The following sources are about the effects of the First World War on German civilians.

**Study the sources carefully and answer the questions which follow.
You should use your own knowledge where appropriate.**

Source C is a German poster from 1918. It has been translated into English.

Source C

BRITAIN'S THE CAUSE!

- WHY ARE WE STILL FIGHTING?
- WHY DO WE HAVE TO SCRIMP AND SAVE?
- WHY CAN'T WE GO ABOUT OUR ORDINARY LIFE IN PEACE?

BECAUSE BRITAIN IS OUR DEADLY ENEMY.

- LET US GO FORWARD IN STRENGTH TOGETHER.
- WE CAN STILL GUARANTEE VICTORY FOR GERMANY.

---

3. What opinions does the poster (**Source C**) want German people to have?   **3**

In **Source D**, the historian, John Keegan, describes Germany during war time.

Source D

> The winter of 1916–1917 became the "turnip winter" when that tasteless and unnutritious root appeared as a substitute or an additive at most meals. Luxuries, particularly coffee, disappeared from the tables of all but the rich. Real necessities like soap were strictly rationed.

4. How fully does **Source D** show the difficulties faced by German civilians in the First World War?

   You should use **your own knowledge** and give reasons for your answer.   **4**

[END OF CONTEXT IIB]

UNIT II—INTERNATIONAL COOPERATION AND CONFLICT

CONTEXT C: 1930s–1960s

SECTION A: KNOWLEDGE AND UNDERSTANDING

Study the information in the sources. You must also use your own knowledge in your answers.

Source A describes Winston Churchill's leadership of Britain in 1940.

Source A

> Churchill took charge of preparations for the defence of Britain. He travelled across miles and miles of coast, inspecting fortifications. He formed a Home Guard of more than a million civilians. His orders streamed out unceasingly.

1. How important was Churchill's leadership to the British war effort in the Second World War? **3**

Source B gives evidence about the atomic bomb dropped on Hiroshima, Japan, on August 6, 1945.

Source B

> There was a glaring, pinkish light in the sky which burned people's eyes out. Anyone within a kilometre of the explosion became a bundle of smoking black charcoal within seconds. Within minutes about 70 000 people were dead.

2. What were the effects of the dropping of the atomic bomb on Hiroshima? **4**

Marks

SECTION B: ENQUIRY SKILLS

The following sources are about the effects of the war on German civilians.

**Study the sources carefully and answer the questions which follow.
You should use your own knowledge where appropriate.**

In **Source C** a German woman living in Hamburg in 1943 describes the aftermath of a British air raid.

Source C

> The following morning all women and children had to be evacuated from the city. It was dreadful. There was no gas, no electricity, not a drop of water. It is hard to imagine the panic and the chaos. We had only one idea: to escape.

3. According to **Source C**, what was the attitude of Germans living in Hamburg towards air raids? 3

Source D is from a leaflet published by German students in Munich in 1943.

Source D

> The war is approaching its certain end. Hitler cannot win the war but only extend it. Germans! Break with everything to do with Nazism before it is too late. A German victory cannot be achieved by criminals. Support the resistance movement; distribute this leaflet.

4. How fully does **Source D** describe the feelings of German civilians during the war?

    You should use **your own knowledge** and give reasons for your answer. 4

[END OF CONTEXT IIC]

UNIT III—PEOPLE AND POWER

CONTEXT A: USA 1850–1880

SECTION A: KNOWLEDGE AND UNDERSTANDING

Study the information in the sources. You must also use your own knowledge in your answers.

In **Source A** a Blackfoot native American chief talks about the importance of land.

Source A

> Our land is more valuable than your white man's money. It will not perish by the flames of fire. As long as the sun shines and the waters flow, this land will be here to give life to men and animals. We cannot sell the lives of men and animals, therefore we cannot sell this land.

1. Describe the attitudes of native Americans ("Indians") to the land.   **3**

Source B is about the causes of the Civil War.

Source B

> A bitter civil war was fought between 1861 and 1865. On one side was the slave-owning South, the Confederate states. They were fighting for the right to manage their own affairs and to opt out of the Union if they wished. On the other side were the Northern states, generally opposed to slavery and determined that America should stay together in one Union.

2. Explain why slavery was a cause of the Civil War.   **3**

Marks

SECTION B: ENQUIRY SKILLS

The following sources are about the activities of the Ku Klux Klan.

Study the sources carefully and answer the questions which follow.

You should use your own knowledge where appropriate.

Source C is a cartoon from a newspaper published in the north of America in 1873.

Source C

WHITE TERRORISM

3. How useful is **Source C** as evidence of the activities of the Ku Klux Klan? 4

4. How fully does **Source C** show what the Ku Klux Klan was like?

   You should use **your own knowledge** and give reasons for your answer. 3

[Turn over

Source D describes some of the methods used by the Ku Klux Klan.

Source D

> The Ku Klux Klan was a secret society set up to terrorise black people. They dressed in ghostly white costumes and carried burning crosses. The Klan often used violence and did not hesitate at torture, arson and murder. Many blacks were hanged without a proper trial. A favourite target was burning the local school which had been opened to give ex slaves and their children a chance to be educated.

5. To what extent do **Sources C** and **D** agree about the treatment of black people after the Civil War? 4

[END OF CONTEXT IIIA]

Marks

UNIT III—PEOPLE AND POWER

CONTEXT B: INDIA 1917–1947

SECTION A: KNOWLEDGE AND UNDERSTANDING

Study the information in the sources. You must also use your own knowledge in your answers.

Source A describes the importance of India to Britain.

Source A

> India had an important role to play in the British Empire. India exported a variety of goods to Britain and in return she was the largest single market for British imports, especially for cotton goods and heavy engineering.

1. Explain why control of India was good for Britain. 3

Source B describes what happened at Amritsar in 1919.

Source B

> In 1919 the British government extended its powers to combat anti-British activities. At Amritsar in the Punjab about 10 000 demonstrators came face to face with British troops in an open space known as the Jallianwalla Bagh which only had one exit. The result was to be known as the Amritsar massacre.

2. Describe the events at Amritsar in April 1919. 3

[Turn over

SECTION B: ENQUIRY SKILLS

The following sources are about Muslim Direct Action.

**Study the sources carefully and answer the questions which follow.
You should use your own knowledge where appropriate.**

Source C is a Muslim League poster from 1946. It shows the areas claimed by Muslims.

Source C

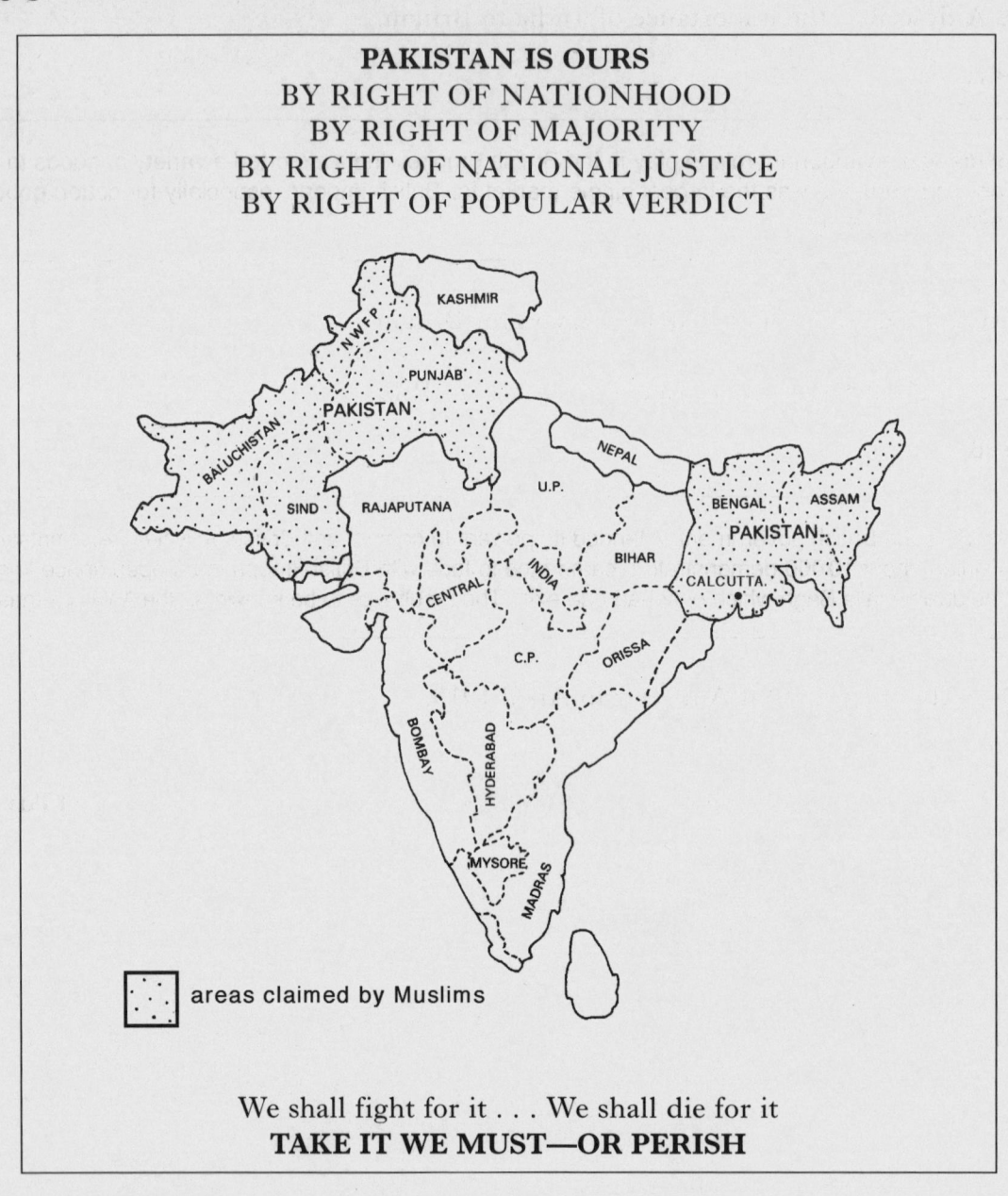

> **PAKISTAN IS OURS**
> **BY RIGHT OF NATIONHOOD**
> **BY RIGHT OF MAJORITY**
> **BY RIGHT OF NATIONAL JUSTICE**
> **BY RIGHT OF POPULAR VERDICT**
>
> [Map of India showing areas claimed by Muslims, including NWFP, Kashmir, Punjab, Baluchistan, Sind (labelled PAKISTAN in the west) and Bengal, Assam (labelled PAKISTAN in the east, with Calcutta)]
>
> areas claimed by Muslims
>
> We shall fight for it . . . We shall die for it
> **TAKE IT WE MUST—OR PERISH**

3. How useful is **Source C** as evidence of Muslim attitudes in 1946?   4

4. How fully does **Source C** reveal the views about partition of people living in India in 1946?

   You should use **your own knowledge** and give reasons for your answer.   3

Marks

In **Source D**, an Indian historian describes Muslim Direct Action Day, August 16th, 1946.

Source D

> Speeches made by some of their leaders encouraged Muslims to fight for Pakistan on Direct Action Day. When the day came, Muslims in Calcutta attacked Hindu shopkeepers, kicked or stabbed them, then smashed and looted their shops. The Hindus retaliated, and in forty-eight hours nearly 5000 people were killed.

5. How far do **Sources C** and **D** agree about Muslim Direct Action?   **4**

[END OF CONTEXT IIIB]

UNIT III—PEOPLE AND POWER

CONTEXT C: RUSSIA 1914–1941

SECTION A: KNOWLEDGE AND UNDERSTANDING

Study the information in the sources. You must also use your own knowledge in your answers.

Source A is about the power of the Russian Tsars.

Source A

> The ruler of Russia was called the Tsar. It was a hereditary title. This meant that when the Tsar died, the crown went to his eldest son. He was chief of the armed forces and head of the Russian Orthodox Church. People obeyed him not just because he was the Tsar but because he had been chosen by God to rule over them.

1. Why were Russian Tsars so powerful? — 3

Source B is taken from a letter by Lenin to the Central Committee of the Bolshevik Party.

Source B

> The truth about Kolchak and Denikin has now been fully revealed. They are responsible for the shooting of tens of thousands of workers, the flogging of peasants in entire districts, and endless looting. Let every worker know what he is fighting for, and what awaits him in the event of a White victory.

2. Describe the ways Russian civilians suffered during the Civil War. — 3

SECTION B: ENQUIRY SKILLS

The following sources are about the New Economic Policy.

**Study the sources carefully and answer the questions which follow.
You should use your own knowledge where appropriate.**

Source C was produced using official Soviet figures released in the late 1920s.

Source C

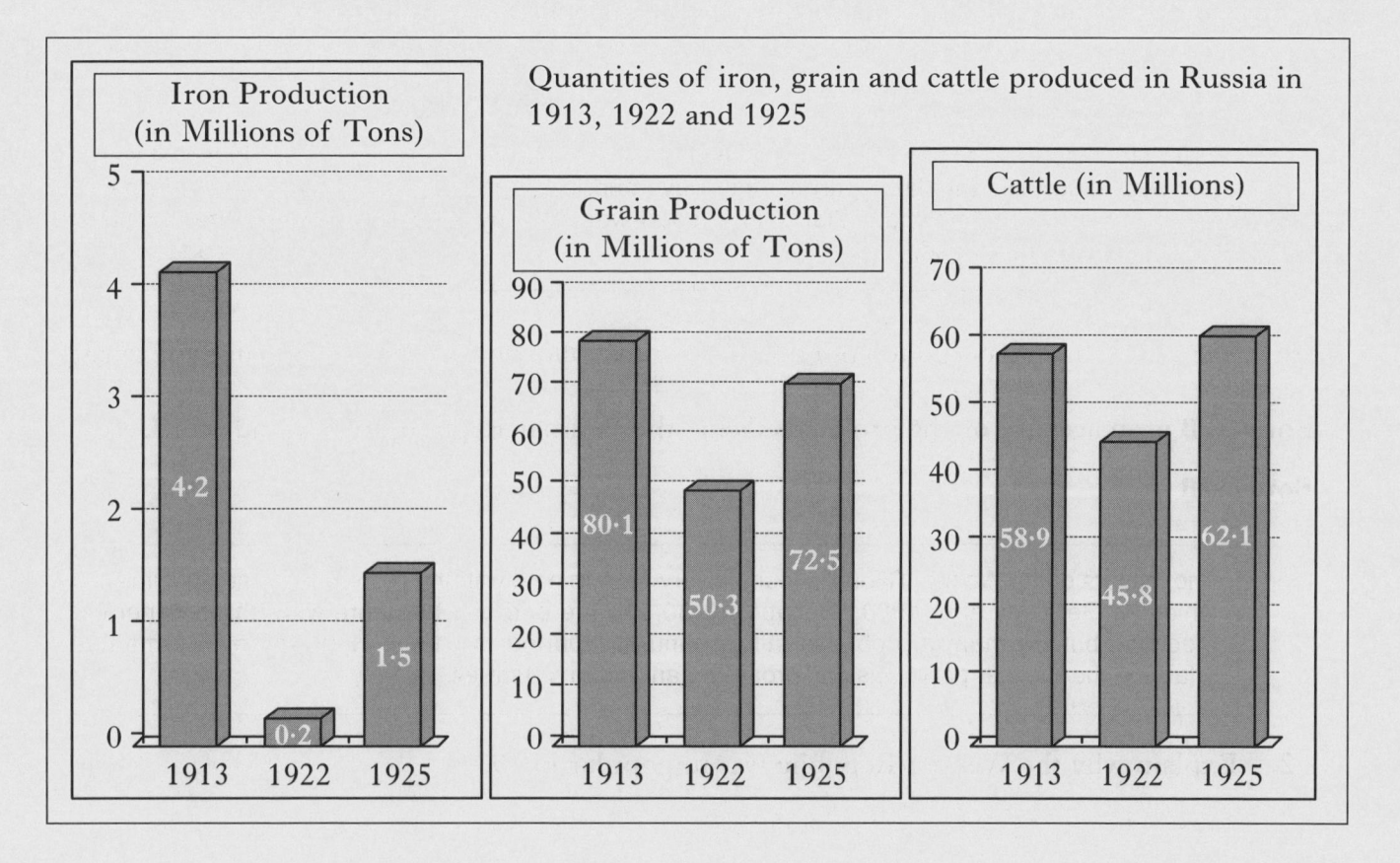

Quantities of iron, grain and cattle produced in Russia in 1913, 1922 and 1925

Iron Production (in Millions of Tons): 1913 – 4.2; 1922 – 0.2; 1925 – 1.5

Grain Production (in Millions of Tons): 1913 – 80.1; 1922 – 50.3; 1925 – 72.5

Cattle (in Millions): 1913 – 58.9; 1922 – 45.8; 1925 – 62.1

3. How useful is **Source C** as evidence of the effects of the New Economic Policy? **4**

4. How fully does **Source C** show the successes of the New Economic Policy?

   You should use **your own knowledge** and give reasons for your answer. **3**

Source D is from "The Russian Revolution" by the historian, J. Quinn.

Source D

> As soon as the peasants became the real owners of the land, they began to work with an enthusiasm previously unknown. By 1925 grain production had increased and was back to the levels of 1913. Animals, which had been largely wiped out during the war, began to reappear in great numbers. Starvation was reduced and industrial production began to climb again.

5. To what extent do **Sources C** and **D** agree about the effects of the New Economic Policy? **4**

[END OF CONTEXT IIIC]

UNIT III—PEOPLE AND POWER

CONTEXT D: GERMANY 1918–1939

SECTION A: KNOWLEDGE AND UNDERSTANDING

Study the information in the sources. You must also use your own knowledge in your answers.

Source A describes Hitler's trial after the 1923 Beer Hall Putsch in Munich.

Source A

> Hitler stood accused of treason. It seemed that his short political career was over. In fact, it was just beginning. His trial lasted twenty-four days and it was front page news in every German newspaper. Everything that Hitler said in court was read by millions of people, the biggest audience he had ever had.

1. Describe what happened to Hitler in the months following the Beer Hall Putsch of 1923. **3**

Source B is an account of the problems facing the Weimar Republic by the end of 1932.

Source B

> The leaders of the Weimar Republic found it very hard to deal with the problems of unemployment which hit Germany after 1929. Between 1930 and the end of 1932 there were three general elections but Germany's problems still continued. During this time, Hitler toured Germany attacking the Weimar politicians and promising an end to Versailles.

2. Explain why the Weimar Republic was unpopular in 1932. **3**

SECTION B: ENQUIRY SKILLS

The following sources are about the Hitler Youth Movement.

**Study the sources carefully and answer the questions which follow.
You should use your own knowledge where appropriate.**

Source C is from a children's colouring book produced by the Nazis in the mid 1930s.

Source C

HITLER YOUTH AT CAMP

3. How useful is **Source C** as evidence of the popularity of the Hitler Youth in Nazi Germany?   **4**

Source D is from a recent textbook describing some of the activities of the Hitler Youth.

Source D

> Many young people were attracted by the exciting and interesting range of activities of the Youth movement. There were many outdoor events such as camping and hiking as well as sports. Some enjoyed the military aspects of the Youth movement: the uniforms; the marching and the discipline. Other young people liked the music that was a frequent part of their military parades.

4. To what extent do **Sources C** and **D** agree on the appeal of the Hitler Youth movement?   **4**

5. How fully does **Source D** describe the ways Nazis attracted young people?

   You should use **your own knowledge** and give reasons for your answer   **3**

[END OF CONTEXT IIID]

[END OF QUESTION PAPER]

2002 GENERAL

1540/402

NATIONAL
QUALIFICATIONS
2002

MONDAY, 20 MAY
10.20 AM – 11.50 AM

HISTORY
STANDARD GRADE
General Level

Answer questions from Unit I **and** Unit II **and** Unit III.

Choose only **one** Context from each Unit and answer Sections A **and** B. The Contexts chosen should be those you have studied.

The Contexts in each Unit are:

Unit I— Changing Life in Scotland and Britain
- Context A: 1750s–1850s .... Pages 2–3
- Context B: 1830s–1930s .... Pages 4–5
- Context C: 1880s–Present Day .... Pages 6–7

Unit II— International Cooperation and Conflict
- Context A: 1790s–1820s .... Pages 8–9
- Context B: 1890s–1920s .... Pages 10–11
- Context C: 1930s–1960s .... Pages 12–13

Unit III— People and Power
- Context A: USA 1850–1880 .... Pages 14–15
- Context B: India 1917–1947 .... Pages 16–17
- Context C: Russia 1914–1941 .... Pages 18–19
- Context D: Germany 1918–1939 .... Pages 20–21

You must use the information in the sources, and your own knowledge, to answer the questions.

Number the questions as shown in the question paper.

Some sources have been adapted or translated.

UNIT I—CHANGING LIFE IN SCOTLAND AND BRITAIN

CONTEXT A: 1750s–1850s

SECTION A: KNOWLEDGE AND UNDERSTANDING

Study the information in the sources. You must also use your own knowledge in your answers.

In **Source A** the historian Simon Mason writes about changes to the population of Britain in the eighteenth century.

Source A

> The death rate fell steeply after 1770 and continued to fall. After 1790 there were still years of bad harvests but nothing approaching a famine. There were plenty of diseases but no epidemics. There was also a definite rise in the standard of living in the eighteenth century.

1. Why did the population of Britain rise in the eighteenth century?   **4**

Source B gives evidence of the changes made in Scotland by the Reform Act of 1832.

Source B

> The Act, though a moderate measure, corrected the worst abuses of the old system. The new voters were shopkeepers and skilled workers in the burghs and wealthy farmers in the counties. If the Radicals still complained that most workers remained voteless, more political power to the middle class was a real advance.

2. Describe the changes brought about by the Reform Act of 1832.   **3**

SECTION B: ENQUIRY SKILLS

The issue for investigating is:

> Changes in agriculture between 1750 and 1850 were good for Scotland.

Study the sources carefully and answer the questions which follow.

You should use your own knowledge where appropriate.

Source C was written in a report by Sir John Sinclair, MP in 1814.

Source C

> The great advantage to Scotland of threshing mills being now so common, is that the amount of manual labour is greatly reduced. Also the quantity of agricultural produce is greatly increased. Managing farming on large estates has become much easier.

3. How useful is **Source C** for investigating the effects of changes in agriculture in Scotland after 1750? **3**

Source D is from "Changing Life in Scotland and Britain" by Craig Madden.

Source D

> Many poorer tenants lost their land and became farm labourers. Many such labourers were later put out of work by the introduction of farm machines and were reduced to begging. Others left the countryside altogether, and found jobs in towns. The tragedy of the disappearance of the small tenant farmer can be seen in the number of deserted villages.

4. What evidence in **Source C** agrees with the view that changes in agriculture were good for Scotland?

   What evidence in **Source D** does **not** agree with the view that changes in agriculture were good for Scotland? **5**

5. How far do you agree that changes in agriculture between 1750 and 1850 were good for Scotland?

   You must use evidence **from the sources** and **your own knowledge** to come to a conclusion. **4**

[END OF CONTEXT IA]

Now turn to the Context you have chosen in Unit II.

UNIT I—CHANGING LIFE IN SCOTLAND AND BRITAIN

CONTEXT B: 1830s–1930s

SECTION A: KNOWLEDGE AND UNDERSTANDING

Study the information in the sources. You must also use your own knowledge in your answers.

In **Source A** the historian Malcolm Falkus discusses population growth in Britain in the period 1830–1880.

Source A

> Earlier historians laid great importance for population growth on medical treatment. Now emphasis is on social factors such as better diet, less overcrowding and greater cleanliness. Less credit is given to the medical profession.

1. Why did the population of Britain grow between 1830 and 1880? **4**

In **Source B** the historian Alastair Gray describes changes in voting in Scotland.

Source B

> In 1868 a Second Reform Act gave skilled workmen the vote and so 230 000 men in Scotland could take part in elections. In 1884, a Third Reform Act was passed. This meant that farm workers, crofters, miners and other working men could now vote.

2. Describe the changes in voting between 1850 and 1930. **3**

Marks

SECTION B: ENQUIRY SKILLS

The issue for investigating is:

> The development of railways between 1850 and 1930 was good for Scotland.

Study the sources carefully and answer the questions which follow.

You should use your own knowledge where appropriate.

Source C was written in "The Railway Magazine" in January 1921.

Source C

> Express trains from Edinburgh and Glasgow make Aberdeen station busy with travellers. During the Glasgow Holiday week of 1920, 15 000 people travelled to Aberdeen. Trains also carry 60 000 tons of fish to English markets. Horses and pedigree cattle are moved by rail from the North East to other parts of the country.

3. How useful is **Source C** for investigating how railways were used in Scotland between 1850 and 1930? **3**

Source D is from "The Scottish Railway Story", published in 1992.

Source D

> There were those who objected to some of the changes which the railway brought in its wake, such as Sunday travel or the pollution of the town or countryside. Sections of the community saw the coming of the railways as a threat, the coach owners understandably.

4. What evidence is there in **Source C** that the development of railways was good for Scotland?

   What evidence is there in **Source D** that the development of railways was **not** good for Scotland? **5**

5. How far do you agree that the development of railways between 1850 and 1930 was good for Scotland?

   You must use evidence **from the sources** and **your own knowledge** to come to a conclusion. **4**

[*END OF CONTEXT IB*]

Now turn to the Context you have chosen in Unit II.

UNIT I—CHANGING LIFE IN SCOTLAND AND BRITAIN

CONTEXT C: 1880s–Present Day

SECTION A: KNOWLEDGE AND UNDERSTANDING

Study the information in the sources. You must also use your own knowledge in your answers.

In **Source A** the historian John Patrick writes about population changes in Britain after 1880.

Source A

> Medical improvements helped to reduce the death rate. Better housing meant there was less chance of disease spreading. People were also living longer because of a healthier diet. At the same time, however, the birth rate had fallen so old people made up a much greater proportion of the population than ever before.

1. Why did the population of Britain continue to grow after 1880? **4**

Source B was said by Lord Birkenhead in 1928.

Source B

> In 1918 I was against the extension of the franchise to women of any age. I am now against the giving of the vote to women over 21 years of age. This all began in 1918 when a Member of Parliament said, "If you are giving the vote to our brave soldiers how about our brave female munition workers as well?"

2. Describe changes in voting between 1900 and 1969. **3**

SECTION B: ENQUIRY SKILLS

The issue for investigating is:

> Developments in road transport in the twentieth century were good for Scotland.

Study the sources carefully and answer the questions which follow.

You should use your own knowledge where appropriate.

In **Source C** a Glasgow resident remembers when the M8 motorway was built in the 1960s.

Source C

> There were streets here, with tenements built at the start of the century. They were very solid houses with good sized bedrooms. Well, a slum order was put on them and we were forced out in 1965 and rehoused in new flats. There was nothing wrong with our old place. The council were just desperate to pull it down for the new, noisy motorway coming through.

3. How useful is **Source C** for investigating the effects of developments in road transport in Scotland? 3

Source D is from a modern history book.

Source D

> Petrol vehicles have brought a great deal of fun and freedom into many people's lives. They have helped bring cheaper goods into the shops. Thousands of Scots make their living from the transport industries. Communities that were once isolated are now within a few hours' reach of Glasgow and Edinburgh.

4. What evidence in **Source C** does **not** agree with the view that developments in road transport were good for Scotland?

   What evidence in **Source D** agrees with the view that developments in road transport were good for Scotland? 5

5. How far do you agree that developments in road transport were good for Scotland?

   You must use evidence **from the sources** and **your own knowledge** to come to a conclusion. 4

[END OF CONTEXT IC]

Now turn to the Context you have chosen in Unit II.

UNIT II—INTERNATIONAL COOPERATION AND CONFLICT

CONTEXT A: 1790s–1820s

SECTION A: KNOWLEDGE AND UNDERSTANDING

Study the information in the sources. You must also use your own knowledge in your answers.

Source A is about the causes of the Revolutionary War.

Source A

> The execution of King Louis XVI appeared to many people in Britain as a barbaric and unjustified act which made the Revolution the enemy of all kings. Prime Minister Pitt protested to the French ambassador in London, and the French reply was a declaration of war.

1. Explain why Britain went to war against France in 1793. **4**

Source B describes an effect of the war on civilians in Britain.

Source B

> The Wars brought misery upon the working classes because of a great rise in the cost of living. Bread in particular rose in price because imports of wheat were difficult to obtain. The price of wheat almost tripled from 1790 to 1812.

2. How serious were problems of food supply for the British people during the wars with France? **3**

SECTION B: ENQUIRY SKILLS

The following sources are about the Fourth Coalition against France, 1813–1814.

Study the sources carefully and answer the questions which follow.

You should use your own knowledge where appropriate.

Source C is a cartoon by the British Artist, James Gilray, published in 1814. It shows Napoleon being attacked on all sides.

Source C

3. How useful is **Source C** as evidence about the Fourth Coalition against France? **4**

In **Source D** the historian H. L. Peacock describes one success of the Fourth Coalition.

Source D

> At Leipzig, the "Battle of the Nations" involving 500 000 men was fought on October 16th–18th, 1813. The allies included Austrians, Prussians, Russians and Swedes. Napoleon, attacked on all sides, was defeated and flung back over the Rhine.

4. How far do **Sources C** and **D** agree about the Fourth Coalition against France? **4**

5. How fully does **Source D** explain why the Fourth Coalition against France was successful?

   You should use **your own knowledge** and give reasons for your answer. **4**

[END OF CONTEXT IIA]

Now turn to the Context you have chosen in Unit III.

UNIT II—INTERNATIONAL COOPERATION AND CONFLICT

CONTEXT B: 1890s–1920s

SECTION A: KNOWLEDGE AND UNDERSTANDING

Study the information in the sources. You must also use your own knowledge in your answers.

Source A is from a modern history textbook by Tony Howarth.

Source A

> On 28 June 1914 the heir to the Austrian throne, Archduke Franz Ferdinand and his wife were shot dead in Sarajevo, the capital of Bosnia. The assassin, Gavrilo Princip, was a Bosnian Serb who wanted Bosnian independence from Austria. But Austria blamed Serbia and used the murders as an excuse to smash Serbian nationalism.

1. Explain why the assassinations at Sarajevo led to the outbreak of the First World War. **4**

Source B is from the war memoirs of British Prime Minister, Lloyd George.

Source B

> The steady improvement in our national health figures during and after the war shows that food rationing did more good than harm. Although there was some scarcity, we were never faced with famine or actual hardship.

2. How serious a problem was rationing for British civilians during the First World War? **3**

SECTION B: ENQUIRY SKILLS

The following sources are about tanks in the First World War.

Study the sources carefully and answer the questions which follow.

You should use your own knowledge where appropriate.

Source C is a photograph from the Imperial War Museum collection of a tank in action in 1916.

Source C

3. How useful is **Source C** as evidence of the use of tanks in the First World War? 4

Source D is from a modern history textbook.

Source D

> The tank had a maximum speed—on a good road—of about six kilometres an hour. It was driven by caterpillar tracks, protected by steel armour and could carry four machine guns. They were to be used against entanglements of barbed wire. Tanks had a crew of eight who had to face many problems.

4. How far do **Sources C** and **D** agree about the tank? 4

Source E was written in the memoirs of Lieutenant F. Mitchell who was in charge of a tank in 1917.

Source E

> The tank that went for the pill box got stuck in the mud. As it sank deeper, it fired desperately. By chance, its six-pounder gun pointed straight inside the pill box door and most of the German garrison of 60 men was killed by the tank's fire. There were only 29 British casualties instead of a thousand. The tank had shown its qualities.

5. How fully does **Source E** describe the use of tanks in the First World War?

   You should use **your own knowledge** and give reasons for your answer. 4

[END OF CONTEXT IIB]

Now turn to the Context you have chosen in Unit III.

UNIT II—INTERNATIONAL COOPERATION AND CONFLICT

CONTEXT C: 1930s–1960s

SECTION A: KNOWLEDGE AND UNDERSTANDING

Study the information in the sources. You must also use your own knowledge in your answers.

Source A describes why Hitler attacked Poland in 1939.

Source A

> Hitler wanted Danzig. The people of Danzig were mainly German. They had been separated from Germany by the "Polish Corridor" in 1919. The Poles refused to give in to Hitler's demands. Soon Hitler was demanding the whole of Western Poland.

1. Explain why Germany attacked Poland in September 1939. **4**

Source B explains the building of the Berlin Wall.

Source B

> When he met John Kennedy in 1961 Khrushchev thought he could dominate him and insisted that America recognise the existence of East Germany. Kennedy refused and America prepared for war. In revenge, the Soviets built a wall right across Berlin.

2. How important was the Berlin crisis of 1961 as a threat to world peace? **3**

Marks

SECTION B: ENQUIRY SKILLS

The following sources are about air raids during the Second World War.

Study the sources carefully and answer the questions which follow.

You should use your own knowledge where appropriate.

Source C is a description of a bombing raid on Clydeside from the Glasgow Herald, 15 May 1941.

Source C

> Houses, churches and schools in the area were wrecked. In this district hardly a pane of glass remained in shop windows. Streets were strewn with broken glass, rubble and debris. People spent yesterday recovering property and furniture from their partially ruined homes and shops.

3. How useful is **Source C** as evidence of the effects of an air raid in the Second World War?   4

Source D shows the aftermath of an air raid on Menzies Road, Aberdeen on August 8th, 1941.

Source D

4. To what extent do **Sources C** and **D** agree about the effects of an air raid?   4

In **Source E** a young Scotswoman describes an air raid in 1941.

Source E

> We heard the wail of the sirens and in the silence after that we could hear the drone of a plane. There was panic as instinct drove us all towards the door and the stairs. Women and girls were white faced and shaking. Then the bombs fell.

5. How fully does the evidence in **Source E** explain what happened in an air raid?

    You should use **your own knowledge** and give reasons for your answer.   4

[END OF CONTEXT IIC]

Now turn to the Context you have chosen in Unit III.

UNIT III—PEOPLE AND POWER

CONTEXT A: USA 1850–1880

SECTION A: KNOWLEDGE AND UNDERSTANDING

Study the information in the sources. You must also use your own knowledge in your answers.

Source A gives evidence about the effects of railroad building on the west.

Source A

> Thousands of farms were created close to the rail routes. On the Great Plains, the railroads gave a great boost to homesteading farmers. Ranching and the cattle industry also benefited from the railroads as animals could be transported easily. Some cities grew large because of the railroads.

1. Describe the effects of the railroads on the west of America. **3**

Source B was printed in a Southern newspaper in 1860.

Source B

> Northerners have robbed us of our property. They have murdered our citizens while they were trying to get our property back. They have ignored the laws of the Supreme Court and now have capped it all by electing Abraham Lincoln as President.

2. Explain why many Southerners were angry with Northerners in 1860. **3**

SECTION B: ENQUIRY SKILLS

The following sources are about relationships between native Americans (Indians) and the US Government.

Study the sources carefully and answer the questions which follow.

You should use your own knowledge where appropriate.

Source C is from a speech given by Red Cloud, a Sioux Chief, to a representative of the US Government in 1866.

Source C

> You are the White Chief who has come to steal the road (the Bozeman Trail). The Great Father (US President) sends us presents and wants us to sell him the road but the White Chief comes with soldiers to steal it before our people say "yes" or "no". I will talk with you no more. I will go now and fight you. As long as I live, I will fight for the last hunting grounds of my people.

3. What is the attitude of Red Cloud towards the American Government? **3**

Source D is taken from "Native Peoples of North America" by Susan Edmonds.

Source D

> The Sioux, fearing a white invasion and the destruction of the buffalo herds, began attacking soldiers on the Bozeman Trail. In 1866 Red Cloud received news that the US Government was planning to build forts along the Trail. After much fighting between the US Army and the Sioux, the government made peace with Red Cloud.

4. How far do **Sources C** and **D** agree about Sioux attitudes to the Bozeman Trail? **3**

[END OF CONTEXT IIIA]

UNIT III—PEOPLE AND POWER

CONTEXT B: INDIA 1917–1947

SECTION A: KNOWLEDGE AND UNDERSTANDING

Study the information in the sources. You must also use your own knowledge in your answers.

In **Source A** a modern historian writes about the Untouchables.

Source A

> The outcasts in Indian society were called Untouchables and they had to do the tasks which other Hindus would not do. They were below the caste system: creatures whose very shadows could contaminate.

1. Explain why life was unpleasant for the Untouchables. 3

Source B is from "The Life of Mahatma Gandhi" by Louis Fischer

Source B

> Some Hindus never forgave Gandhi for his love of Untouchables. But to vast multitudes he was the Mahatma. They asked his blessing; they were happy to touch his feet; they kissed the ground where he passed.

2. Describe the different views of Gandhi held by Indians. 3

Marks

SECTION B: ENQUIRY SKILLS

The following sources are about the events at Amritsar in 1919.

Study the sources carefully and answer the questions which follow.

You should use your own knowledge where appropriate.

Source C is from the Hunter Report into the events at Amritsar on April 13th, 1919.

Source C

> As soon as General Dyer arrived he entered with his troops. Without giving the crowd any warning he ordered his troops to fire. The firing continued for about ten minutes. There is no evidence of the kind of speech the audience was listening to. None of them had any firearms. The soldiers fired 1650 rounds of ammunition. The crowd was a perfect target.

3. What did the author of the Hunter Report think about the actions of General Dyer?   **3**

Source D was written by the historian J. Simkin.

Source D

> General Dyer sent town criers round Amritsar to inform the people that all public meetings were banned. It was later discovered that his orders were not read in places where most people would hear them. When Dyer heard about a meeting he took ninety soldiers and immediately gave instructions for them to fire into the defenceless crowd until they ran out of ammunition. No warning was given and when the riflemen had finished, 379 Indians lay dead.

4. In what ways do **Sources C** and **D** agree about events at Amritsar?   **3**

[END OF CONTEXT IIIB]

UNIT III—PEOPLE AND POWER

CONTEXT C: RUSSIA 1914–1941

SECTION A: KNOWLEDGE AND UNDERSTANDING

Study the information in the sources. You must also use your own knowledge in your answers.

In **Source A**, a modern historian describes events in February, 1917.

Source A

> Demonstrations broke out in Petrograd. Women protesting about food shortages were supported by striking factory workers. To make matters worse, troops sent to stop the disturbances mutinied.

1. Describe the main events of the February Revolution. **3**

In **Source B** a kulak explains his opposition to Stalin's collectivisation policy.

Source B

> Whoever heard of such a thing—to give up our land and our animals; to hand over our tools and our farm buildings; to work all the time and divide everything with others?

2. Why did the kulaks oppose Stalin's plans to collectivise Russian agriculture? **3**

SECTION B: ENQUIRY SKILLS

The following sources are about the situation in Russia at the start of the Civil War in 1918.

Study the sources carefully and answer the questions which follow.

You should use your own knowledge where appropriate.

In **Source C** Bukharin, a member of the Bolshevik Government, describes their White opponents.

Source C

> There can be no question of freedom for our opponents. The Bolshevik Party does not allow freedom of the press or freedom of speech for them. They are the enemies of the people. The Party must ruthlessly put down all attempts by our White opponents to return to power. We alone maintain order.

3. What did Bukharin think of opponents of the Bolshevik Party?   3

Source D is from a speech by Kaledin, leader of the Don Cossacks, in early 1918.

Source D

> The Cossacks consider the acts of the Bolsheviks to be criminal and ruthless. Until the return of the Provisional Government to power and the restoration of law and order in Russia, I have taken on myself all power in the Don region.

4. How far do **Sources C** and **D** agree about the Bolsheviks and their actions?   3

[END OF CONTEXT IIIC]

UNIT III—PEOPLE AND POWER

CONTEXT D: GERMANY 1918–1939

SECTION A: KNOWLEDGE AND UNDERSTANDING

Study the information in the sources. You must also use your own knowledge in your answers.

Source A is from a report by the Mayor of Berlin in 1923.

Source A

> Many children, even the youngest, never get a drop of milk and come to school without a warm breakfast. The children frequently have no shirt or warm clothing. Terrible poverty gradually weakens any sense of cleanliness and leaves room only for thoughts of the struggle against hunger and cold.

1. Describe some of the problems faced by Germans during the period of hyperinflation in 1923. **3**

Source B is about the support Hitler enjoyed during the 1930s.

Source B

> Hitler was popular because he was successful. He gave a strong lead after years of weak government and social conflict. Through the use of rallies and ceremonial events the Nazis kept up an image of confidence and purpose.

2. Why was Hitler so popular with many Germans in the 1930s? **3**

Marks

SECTION B: ENQUIRY SKILLS

The following sources are about Hitler's attitude to the Jews.

Study the sources carefully and answer the questions which follow.
You should use your own knowledge where appropriate.

Source C is from a speech made by Hitler in 1922.

Source C

> The Jews are a people of robbers. They have never founded civilisation, though they have destroyed civilisations by the hundred. They have created nothing of their own. They have no art of their own but bit by bit they have stolen it from other people. They have watched them at work and then made their copies.

3. What was Hitler's attitude towards the Jews?   **3**

In **Source D** a modern historian describes Hitler's attitude towards the Jews.

Source D

> Hitler believed that Aryan superiority was being threatened by the Jewish race. He argued that they were lazy and had contributed little to world civilisation. According to Hitler, Jews were responsible for everything he did not like, including modern art. He also claimed that Jews had been responsible for Germany losing the First World War.

4. How far do **Sources C** and **D** agree about Hitler's attitude to the Jews?   **3**

[END OF CONTEXT IIID]

[END OF QUESTION PAPER]

[BLANK PAGE]

2003 GENERAL

Official SQA Past Papers: General History 2003

G

1540/402

NATIONAL QUALIFICATIONS 2003

MONDAY, 12 MAY 10.20 AM – 11.50 AM

HISTORY STANDARD GRADE
General Level

Answer questions from Unit I **and** Unit II **and** Unit III.

Choose only **one** Context from each Unit and answer Sections A **and** B. The Contexts chosen should be those you have studied.

The Contexts in each Unit are:

　　Unit I— Changing Life in Scotland and Britain
　　　　Context A: 1750s–1850s .... Pages 2–3
　　　　Context B: 1830s–1930s .... Pages 4–5
　　　　Context C: 1880s–Present Day .... Pages 6–7

　　Unit II— International Cooperation and Conflict
　　　　Context A: 1790s–1820s .... Pages 8–9
　　　　Context B: 1890s–1920s .... Pages 10–11
　　　　Context C: 1930s–1960s .... Pages 12–13

　　Unit III— People and Power
　　　　Context A: USA 1850–1880 .... Pages 14–15
　　　　Context B: India 1917–1947 .... Pages 16–17
　　　　Context C: Russia 1914–1941 .... Pages 18–19
　　　　Context D: Germany 1918–1939 .... Pages 20–21

You must use the information in the sources, and your own knowledge, to answer the questions.

Number the questions as shown in the question paper.

Some sources have been adapted or translated.

UNIT I—CHANGING LIFE IN SCOTLAND AND BRITAIN

CONTEXT A: 1750s–1850s

SECTION A: KNOWLEDGE AND UNDERSTANDING

Study the information in the sources. You must also use your own knowledge in your answers.

Source A describes work in a cotton mill.

Source A

> Factory employment was very different. Costly machinery had to be used on a continuous basis and that meant long hours and a strict supervision of labour. In the cotton mills, even night work was not unknown when trade was brisk. Workers normally laboured for six days a week.

1. Describe working conditions in a cotton mill. **4**

Source B is about farm housing from the memoirs of Dr James Russell.

Source B

> The cottages for the shepherds in the Scottish Borders were little better than dark, smoky hovels. Their walls were made of stone and turf and their floor of earth. A hole in the middle of the roof was the only chimney and rain or snow sometimes entered this open space.

2. How serious a problem was poor housing for farming families in Lowland and Border Scotland? **3**

SECTION B: ENQUIRY SKILLS

The issue for investigating is:

> The Clearances brought benefits for the evicted Highlanders.

Study the sources carefully and answer the questions which follow.

You should use your own knowledge where appropriate.

Source C is by Patrick Sellar who was factor of the Sutherland estates in the early nineteenth century.

Source C

> Look inside one of the newly built fishermen's cottages, where the evicted Highlanders have been settled, and you will see the man and his wife and his young children weaving their nets around the winter fire. Contrast that with the poverty and filth of an unevicted tenant's turf hut. You cannot say that these men have been injured by civilisation. They are well off.

3. How useful is **Source C** for investigating the effects of the Highland Clearances?   3

Source D was written by the Rev. Donald Sage who witnessed a clearance.

Source D

> It was the month of April, 1819, that they were all on one day to quit their cottages and go. For some, a few miserable patches of ground were given out as plots, without anything in the shape of the poorest hut to shelter them. Upon these plots it was decided that they should farm the ground and occupy themselves as fishermen, although the great majority had never set foot in a boat in their lives.

4. What evidence in **Source C** agrees with the view that the Clearances brought benefits for the evicted Highlanders?

   What evidence in **Source D** suggests that life for evicted Highlanders was not good?   5

5. How far do you agree that the Clearances brought benefits for the evicted Highlanders?

   You must use evidence **from the sources** and **your own knowledge** to come to a conclusion.   4

[END OF CONTEXT 1A]

Now turn to the Context you have chosen in Unit II.

UNIT I—CHANGING LIFE IN SCOTLAND AND BRITAIN

CONTEXT B: 1830s–1930s

SECTION A: KNOWLEDGE AND UNDERSTANDING

Study the information in the sources. You must also use your own knowledge in your answers.

Source A is an eyewitness account of farming improvements in East Lothian in the nineteenth century.

Source A

> There was hardly any waste ground. It was all planted with crops. All the fields were straight and tidy looking. I had never seen anything like it. Red roofed steadings with smoke coming from their chimneys was evidence that threshing was taking place. Every farm had its steam engine and threshing machinery.

1. Describe the changes which had taken place in farming in the nineteenth century. **4**

Source B is about housing in a rural area in the late nineteenth century.

Source B

> In the countryside, rows of reasonably solid stone or brick cottages appeared on almost every farm. They would each have a stone or a wooden floor and a fireplace. Before long, they would also all have running water.

2. How important were the improvements made to rural housing by the late nineteenth century? **3**

Marks

SECTION B: ENQUIRY SKILLS

The issue for investigating is:

> The Scots who emigrated in the nineteenth century had a better standard of living than at home.

Study the sources carefully and answer the questions which follow.

You should use your own knowledge where appropriate.

Source C was written by Simon Fraser who emigrated to Australia from Inverness. It was published in the "Inverness Courier" in 1854.

Source C

> Tell all to come here where they get good wages and not to be starving at home as they do. I was at Melbourne and was offered £10 per week but I hope to get £12 per week. This is the country to live in. In six months I will be an independent man. Everyone that works hard will do well here.

3. How useful is **Source C** for investigating emigration from Scotland during the nineteenth century? 3

Source D is taken from a letter sent by a Scotsman who emigrated to Australia in the nineteenth century.

Source D

> My daughter has got a job working for a minister for only £10 a year. I could have got her a job with me but I would not allow it, the flour mill being a dangerous place to work. My wages are ten shillings (50p) a week. I work from 6 am until 8 pm. The people here are wishing for rain as it has not rained for seven months. This country is not as good as made out at home.

4. What evidence in **Source C** supports the view that Scots who emigrated had a better standard of living?

   What evidence in **Source D** opposes the view that Scots who emigrated had a better standard of living? 5

5. How far do you agree that the Scots who emigrated in the nineteenth century had a better standard of living than at home?

   You must use evidence **from the sources** and **your own knowledge** to come to a conclusion. 4

[*END OF CONTEXT 1B*]

Now turn to the Context you have chosen in Unit II.

UNIT I—CHANGING LIFE IN SCOTLAND AND BRITAIN

CONTEXT C: 1880s–Present Day

SECTION A: KNOWLEDGE AND UNDERSTANDING

Study the information in the sources. You must also use your own knowledge in your answers.

Source A describes the development of trade unions in the early twentieth century.

Source A

> Improving working conditions were partly due to the better organised and more numerous trade unions of the time. In the early twentieth century many small unions combined to form bigger unions. What had once been only Scottish unions sometimes merged with English ones.

1. Describe the changes in trade unions in the early twentieth century. **4**

Source B is about rural housing in Caithness in the early twentieth century.

Source B

> They had no piped water supply. Rain or well water was used. There was no indoor sanitation or even an outdoor toilet. Some favourite corner on the hill or in a quarry was used by both men and women. Nor was there a proper bath. A big wooden tub used for the annual washing of blankets could be used for this purpose.

2. How serious a problem was poor rural housing in the early twentieth century? **3**

SECTION B: ENQUIRY SKILLS

The issue for investigating is:

> Poverty was the main reason why Scots emigrated after 1880.

Study the sources carefully and answer the questions which follow.

You should use your own knowledge where appropriate.

Source C is from a magazine, the "Northern Commercial Journal", published in 1927.

Source C

> One only has to look at the long queues at the Labour Exchange and to read of the many poor, able bodied men who have been given help from the Parish Poor Fund, to know that Fraserburgh has not been flourishing this year. Another sign of the bad times is the steady stream of young men and women to lands beyond the seas in search of a livelihood.

3. How useful is **Source C** for investigating why Scots emigrated in the twentieth century? **3**

Source D is from "Change in Scotland 1830–1930".

Source D

> People left the country, not because they were pushed, but because they were pulled. Scotland had never been a rich country. Other lands offered the promise of cheap farmland, work for all and the prospect of wealth. Right up to the present day, many skilled Scots have gone abroad in search of jobs.

4. What evidence is there in **Source C** that poverty was a reason for Scots emigrating?

   What evidence is there in **Source D** that there were other reasons for Scots emigrating? **5**

5. How far do you agree that poverty was the main reason why Scots emigrated after 1880?

   You must use evidence **from the sources** and **your own knowledge** to come to a conclusion. **4**

[END OF CONTEXT IC]

Now turn to the Context you have chosen in Unit II.

Marks

UNIT II—INTERNATIONAL COOPERATION AND CONFLICT

CONTEXT A: 1790s–1820s

SECTION A: KNOWLEDGE AND UNDERSTANDING

Study the information in the sources. You must also use your own knowledge in your answers.

Source A gives evidence about the outbreak of war between Britain and France.

Source A

> In November 1792 the French issued the Edict of Fraternity, calling on all people to overthrow their rulers, just as they had done. The British government's attitude grew much colder towards France: soon they would be at war.

1. Explain why the Edict of Fraternity helped to bring about the war between Britain and France.   **3**

Source B was written by Robert Hay about his experiences in 1811.

Source B

> The Press Gang took me on board a man-o-war and questioned me. "Are you willing to join the King's Service?" I replied, "No, I can get much better conditions and higher wages in the merchant service and, should I be unable to agree with the Captain, I am free to leave the ship at the end of the voyage."

2. Describe life in the British navy during the wars with France.   **3**

SECTION B: ENQUIRY SKILLS

The following sources are about the Congress of Vienna.

Study the sources carefully and answer the questions which follow.
You should use your own knowledge where appropriate.

Source C is from "A New European Balance" by Stephanie Verbeure.

Source C

> Metternich was wrong when he said the Congress of Vienna had redrawn the map of Europe "for all time". The Congress reflected the wishes of the great powers and ignored the national hopes of many people, Italians and Belgians amongst others. This led to trouble in the future. However, the Congress can be praised for not treating defeated France too harshly.

3. What does the author of **Source C** think about the Congress of Vienna? **4**

Source D comes from "Modern British History" by Norman Lowe.

Source D

> The major success of the Congress was that there was no major conflict in Europe until 1854. On the other hand, there were criticisms of the settlement. It ignored the principle of nationalism: the people of Belgium were placed under Dutch rule and Italians under Austrian rule. They were placed under foreign governments to suit the wishes of the great powers.

4. How far do **Sources C** and **D** agree about the Congress of Vienna? **4**

[END OF CONTEXT IIA]

Now turn to the Context you have chosen in Unit III.

UNIT II—INTERNATIONAL COOPERATION AND CONFLICT

CONTEXT B: 1890s–1920s

SECTION A: KNOWLEDGE AND UNDERSTANDING

Study the information in the sources. You must also use your own knowledge in your answers.

Source A gives evidence about the Balkans before World War One.

Source A

> Different nationalities were mixed together in the Balkans. Two great powers, Russia and Austria-Hungary, bordered the countries in this region. Both wanted to control the area because it gave them access to the Mediterranean sea.

1. Explain why the situation in the Balkans was a cause of tension in Europe before 1914. **3**

Source B is about conditions on the Western Front.

Source B

> The trenches stretched from the Swiss Alps to the English Channel. In these trenches, soldiers were often knee-deep in mud. Many were drowned when they slipped into flooded shell holes. When the temperature dropped they suffered from frost-bite.

2. Describe conditions for soldiers in the trenches on the Western Front. **3**

Marks

SECTION B: ENQUIRY SKILLS

The following sources are about Allied attitudes towards Germany at the end of the war.

Study the sources carefully and answer the questions which follow.

You should use your own knowledge where appropriate.

Source C describes French Prime Minister Clemenceau's views about the Germans in 1918.

Source C

> A German only understands threats. In addition, Germans are without mercy. Therefore you must never negotiate with a German or compromise with him; you must dictate to him otherwise he will not respect you.

3. What does Clemenceau think about the Germans? 4

In **Source D** a British army officer describes his attitude towards the Germans in 1918.

Source D

> The Germans are the most civilised and the most aggressive of European nations. To keep them down for ever would be a hopeless and dangerous task. They will react violently to anything they think is unjust. The Germans should not be treated as underdogs.

4. How far do **Sources C** and **D** agree about the Germans in 1918? 4

[END OF CONTEXT IIB]

Now turn to the Context you have chosen in Unit III.

UNIT II—INTERNATIONAL COOPERATION AND CONFLICT

CONTEXT C: 1930s–1960s

SECTION A: KNOWLEDGE AND UNDERSTANDING

Study the information in the sources. You must also use your own knowledge in your answers.

Source A is about the events following the Czech Crisis in 1938.

Source A

> Chamberlain's hopes of peace did not survive the winter. As soon as the Czech situation was settled, the German government started pressurising the Poles to force them to agree to the return of Danzig to Germany. At the beginning of 1939 Hitler stepped up the campaign to bring about the complete breakup of Czechoslovakia.

1. Explain in what ways the events after the Czech Crisis increased the tension in Europe. **3**

Source B is from the diary of someone living in Hiroshima when the atomic bomb was dropped.

Source B

> Hundreds of people who were trying to escape to the hills passed our house. The sight of them was almost unbearable. Their faces and hands were burnt and swollen. Sheets of skin had peeled away from their bodies and hung down like rags on a scarecrow.

2. Describe the effects which the atomic bomb had on Japanese civilians. **3**

Marks

SECTION B: ENQUIRY SKILLS

The following sources are about the impact of the United Nations.

Study the sources carefully and answer the questions which follow.

You should use your own knowledge where appropriate.

Source C is from "The United Nations" written by Patrick Rooke in 1966.

Source C

> There have been times when the future of the United Nations looked doubtful. However, the United Nations has proved its value and strength. There have been a number of minor, localised wars, some of which threatened to become major wars, but general peace has been maintained in the world. Today, the United Nations is more firmly established than at any time in its history.

3. What did Patrick Rooke think of the United Nations in 1966?   4

In **Source D** Robert Doig describes the progress made by the United Nations up to the 1960s.

Source D

> The initial hopes and plans for the United Nations have been largely achieved since its formation in 1945. No large scale war has threatened the peace of the world and much valuable development work has been completed in many countries by United Nations organisations. There have been tensions between nations and the United Nations has had to deal with them.

4. How far do **Sources C** and **D** agree about the United Nations?   4

[END OF CONTEXT IIC]

Now turn to the Context you have chosen in Unit III.

UNIT III—PEOPLE AND POWER

CONTEXT A: USA 1850–1880

SECTION A: KNOWLEDGE AND UNDERSTANDING

Study the information in the sources. You must also use your own knowledge in your answers.

Source A was written by someone who was worried about the effects of westward expansion.

Source A

> With the stream of emigration westwards, the buffalo will dwindle away. The wandering tribes who depend on them for support will be broken and scattered. The Indians (native Americans) will soon be ruined by whisky and controlled by military posts.

1. Explain some of the ways native Americans (Indians) were affected by westward expansion. 3

Source B is from Abraham Lincoln's Inaugural Address of 1861.

Source B

> I hold the view that the Union of the States is perpetual. It is impossible to destroy it except by some action not provided for in the Constitution itself. If the Union is a contract between States then that contract cannot be broken by less than all the parties who made it. Any act of violence by one State against the authority of the United States is considered a revolutionary act.

2. How important was the Union to Abraham Lincoln? 4

SECTION B: ENQUIRY SKILLS

The following sources are about slavery and the causes of the Civil War.

Study the sources carefully and answer the questions which follow.

You should use your own knowledge where appropriate.

Source C is an advertisement for a runaway slave which was published in a newspaper before the Civil War.

Source C

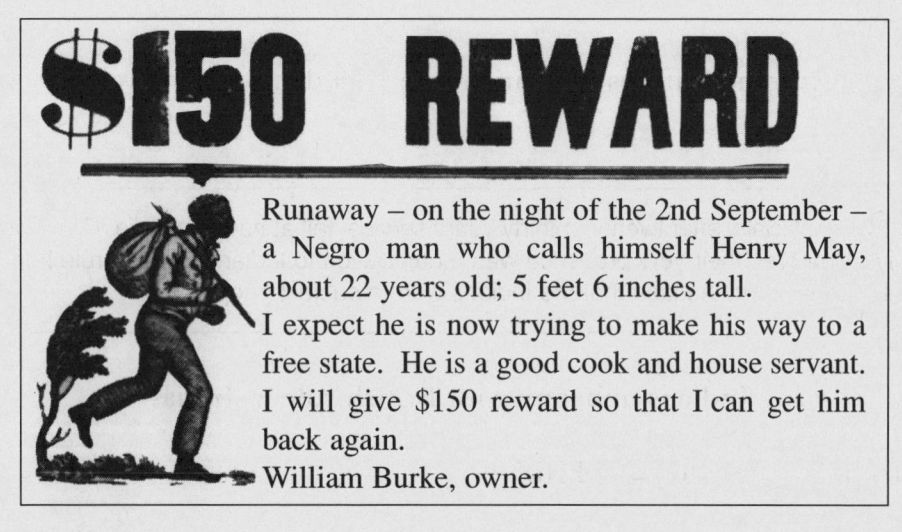

> **$150 REWARD**
>
> Runaway – on the night of the 2nd September – a Negro man who calls himself Henry May, about 22 years old; 5 feet 6 inches tall.
> I expect he is now trying to make his way to a free state. He is a good cook and house servant. I will give $150 reward so that I can get him back again.
> William Burke, owner.

3. How useful is **Source C** as evidence of the evils of slavery? **4**

Source D describes the views contained in anti-slavery petitions.

Source D

> The message of the Abolitionists was always the same. Slavery was a sin and those involved in slavery were sinners who must seek forgiveness immediately. Anyone who refused to speak out against slavery was seen by Abolitionists to be very cowardly.

4. According to the author of **Source D**, what did Abolitionists think about those who did not oppose slavery? **3**

Source E is from www.encartaencyclopedia.com

Source E

> The chief cause of the American Civil War was slavery. Southern States depended on slavery to support their economy and were alarmed at any attacks on it. Opponents of slavery were concerned about the expansion of slavery because they did not want to compete against slave labour.

5. How fully does **Source E** explain the causes of the Civil War?

   You must use evidence **from the source** and **your own knowledge** to come to a conclusion. **3**

[END OF CONTEXT IIIA]

UNIT III—PEOPLE AND POWER

CONTEXT B: INDIA 1917–1947

SECTION A: KNOWLEDGE AND UNDERSTANDING

Study the information in the sources. You must also use your own knowledge in your answers.

Source A is about some features of British rule in India.

Source A

> Many British officials, after twenty or thirty years service, felt at home in India. They were even devoted to India. However, their very presence was a humiliation to Indians. British rule hurt Indian pride and always strengthened the idea that the Indians were a subject people.

1. Why were many Indians unhappy with British rule in India? 3

Source B describes the role of Nehru.

Source B

> Nehru dedicated his life to the nationalist struggle. He spent nine years in nine different jails. He broadened the appeal of Congress and maintained unity in the party. In one vital respect he had to admit failure. The dream that India would become free and remain united was shattered when independence came.

2. How important was Nehru in the struggle for Indian independence? 4

SECTION B: ENQUIRY SKILLS

The sources below are about Gandhi and unrest in India during British rule.

Study the sources carefully and answer the questions which follow.

You should use your own knowledge where appropriate.

Source C is a newspaper photograph taken in 1930 of Mahatma Gandhi and his supporters on the Salt March.

Source C

3. How useful is **Source C** as evidence of Gandhi's protests against British rule? **4**

In **Source D** Gandhi talks about his discontent with the cotton industry in England.

Source D

> Machinery in the past has made us dependent on England. The only way we can rid ourselves of that dependence is to boycott all cloth made by English machinery. That is why we have made it the patriotic duty of every Indian to spin his own cotton. This is our form of attacking a powerful nation like England.

4. What was Gandhi's attitude towards the production of cotton? **3**

Source E is from a biography of Mahatma Gandhi.

Source E

> In the 1920s Gandhi went all over India spreading the message that non-cooperation would lead to independence. At huge public meetings he urged the people to give up wearing foreign clothing and to boycott British cloth. In 1929 he started a new campaign of civil disobedience.

5. How fully does **Source E** describe the tactics used by Gandhi in the campaign for Indian independence?

    Use evidence **from the source** and **your own knowledge** in your answer. **3**

[END OF CONTEXT IIIB]

UNIT III—PEOPLE AND POWER

CONTEXT C: RUSSIA 1914–1941

SECTION A: KNOWLEDGE AND UNDERSTANDING

Study the information in the sources. You must also use your own knowledge in your answers.

Source A is from "Russia and the USSR, 1905–1956".

Source A

> Tsar Nicholas II ruled over a huge empire. He decided everything relating to Russia's government and the armed forces. The people of Russia had no say in the running of the country. Nicholas received advice from a Committee of Ministers—all of whom were chosen from the nobility by the Tsar himself.

1. Explain some of the reasons why many Russians disliked the Tsar before 1914. **3**

Source B is from "Modern World History".

Source B

> The Whites lacked one single leader. Their generals were jealous of each other and refused to attack at the same time. Some White leaders were cruel and this encouraged many Russians to support the Reds.

2. How important was the problem of poor leadership in explaining why the Whites were defeated by the Reds? **4**

SECTION B: ENQUIRY SKILLS

The following sources are about the problems and downfall of the Provisional Government.

Study the sources carefully and answer the questions which follow.

You should use your own knowledge where appropriate.

Source C was said by a Russian soldier in the autumn of 1917.

Source C

> Show me what we are fighting this war for. Is it for democracy or for the capitalist plunderers? If you can prove to me that I am defending the Revolution then I'll go out and fight—without the threat of a death sentence to force me! When the land belongs to the peasants, and the factories to the workers, and the power to the Soviets, then I'll know we have something to fight for. Then we will fight for it!

3. What does the soldier in **Source C** think about continuing to fight in the war? **3**

Source D is a photograph of women queuing for food in Petrograd in September 1917.

Source D

4. How useful is **Source D** as evidence of hardship during the time of the Provisional Government? **4**

Source E is from a modern history textbook.

Source E

> Lenin had spent many years preparing the Bolsheviks for Revolution. He soon became aware that soldiers and civilians disliked the World War. By 1917 he had a small group of dedicated revolutionaries ready and able to seize power. Support for the Bolsheviks increased due to Lenin's slogans.

5. How fully does **Source E** describe the part played by Lenin in the Bolshevik Revolution?

   Use evidence **from the source** and **your own knowledge** in your answer. **3**

[END OF CONTEXT IIIC]

UNIT III—PEOPLE AND POWER

CONTEXT D: GERMANY 1918–1939

SECTION A: KNOWLEDGE AND UNDERSTANDING

Study the information in the sources. You must also use your own knowledge in your answers.

Source A is about the response in Germany to the Versailles Peace Settlement.

Source A

> There was angry reaction in Germany to the Treaty of Versailles. This was not just because they had been forced to accept the treaty and the punishments it contained. They were angry because many Germans would now have to live under foreign rule and because German-speaking Austria was not allowed to join with Germany.

1. Why were many Germans unhappy with the Versailles Peace Settlement? **3**

Source B describes the use of propaganda by the Nazis in the 1930s.

Source B

> The Nazis tried to control all forms of expression and communication. This was done through propaganda and censorship. In overall charge of propaganda was Goebbels who headed the Nazi Ministry of People's Enlightenment and Propaganda, set up in 1933. He controlled the media to spread the Nazi message. Those who ignored the message were made to suffer.

2. How important was Goebbels' propaganda work in controlling the German people? **4**

SECTION B: ENQUIRY SKILLS   Marks

The following sources are about discontent during the time of the Weimar Republic.

Study the sources carefully and answer the questions which follow.
You should use your own knowledge where appropriate.

Source C shows workers collecting their wages in washing baskets during the hyperinflation crisis of 1923.

Source C

3. How useful is **Source C** as evidence of the problems of hyperinflation?   4

Source D was written by a German in 1932.

Source D

> By supporting National Socialism we were showing our hatred of parliamentary politics and democratic debate. We showed we were against all the higgling and haggling of the other parties, their coalitions and their confusions. It was a common man's rejection of "the rascals". The cry was "Throw them all out."

4. What was the attitude of the author of **Source D** towards political parties in Germany?   3

Source E describes the situation in Germany in the early 1930s.

Source E

> The effects of the 1929 Wall Street Crash were keenly felt into the 1930s. As unemployment grew and the dole queues lengthened, so many Germans grew more and more angry with the Weimar politicians. Increasingly, the promises of Hitler proved attractive to many Germans and they turned in their thousands to the Nazis.

5. How fully does **Source E** show why German people turned against the Weimar politicians in the 1930s?

   Use evidence **from the source** and **your own knowledge** in your answer.   3

[END OF CONTEXT IIID]

[END OF QUESTION PAPER]

[BLANK PAGE]

2001 CREDIT

1540/403

NATIONAL QUALIFICATIONS 2001

WEDNESDAY, 30 MAY 10.50 AM – 12.35 PM

HISTORY
STANDARD GRADE
Credit Level

Answer questions from Unit I **and** Unit II **and** Unit III.

Choose only **one** Context from each Unit and answer Sections A **and** B. The Contexts chosen should be those you have studied.

The Contexts in each Unit are:

Unit I— Changing Life in Scotland and Britain
    Context A: 1750s–1850s .... Pages 2–3
    Context B: 1830s–1930s .... Pages 4–5
    Context C: 1880s–Present Day .... Pages 6–7

Unit II— International Cooperation and Conflict
    Context A: 1790s–1820s .... Pages 8–9
    Context B: 1890s–1920s .... Pages 10–11
    Context C: 1930s–1960s .... Pages 12–13

Unit III— People and Power
    Context A: USA 1850–1880.......................... Pages 14–15
    Context B: India 1917–1947 .... Pages 16–17
    Context C: Russia 1914–1941 .... Pages 18–19
    Context D: Germany 1918–1939 .... Pages 20–21

Number the questions as shown in the question paper.

Some sources have been adapted or translated.

Marks

UNIT I—CHANGING LIFE IN SCOTLAND AND BRITAIN

CONTEXT A: 1750s–1850s

SECTION A: KNOWLEDGE AND UNDERSTANDING

> The growth of the cotton industry was made possible by a technological revolution.

1. Describe the new technology which made possible the mass production of cotton. **4**

> In Scotland's industrial towns the solution to overcrowding was to build tall tenement buildings.

2. Do you agree that Scotland's urban housing problems were solved by the building of tenements? Explain your answer. **4**

SECTION B: ENQUIRY SKILLS

The issue for investigating is:

> Radical action in 1820 was a major factor in the struggle for political reform in Scotland.

Study the sources carefully and answer the questions which follow.
You should use your own knowledge where appropriate.

Source A is from "A History of Scotland" by Professor Rosalind Mitchison, published in 1987.

Source A

> The year 1820 witnessed the pathetic incidents of the Radical War. These included a minor skirmish at Bonnymuir which ended in some casualties and three executions. The alarm these events caused left the authorities looking rather foolish. The newspapers pressed home the situation and the discussions which followed were influential in changing Scotland's political situation.

Source B is from the speech made by the Radical, James Wilson, at his trial in Glasgow in 1820.

Source B

> For my part (in Radical activities) you may condemn me to hanging and mutilation but you cannot destroy what I stand for. I am a pioneer in the forefront of freedom's battles. I have attempted to free my country from political shame and weakness. My conscience tells me that I have only done my duty. Your brief authority will soon cease but my actions will be recorded in history.

Source C is from "A History of the Scottish People" by T. C. Smout.

Source C

> One group of marchers fled after a short fight at Bonnymuir in which four Radicals were wounded. Out of all the number of Radical prisoners taken in 1820, only three were executed—one of them, James Wilson, a weaver, on scandalously slender grounds. Some were transported but most of the remainder were released largely because of the reluctance of juries to find anyone guilty. On the coming of better conditions for working men, agitation decreased throughout the country.

3. How useful are **Sources A** and **B** for investigating whether Radical action was a major factor in the struggle for political reform in Scotland? **4**

4. What evidence is there in the sources to support the view that Radical action was a major factor in the struggle for political reform in Scotland?

   What evidence in the sources suggests that Radical action was **not** a major factor in the struggle for political reform in Scotland? **6**

5. How important was Radical action in 1820 in the struggle for political reform in Scotland?

   You must use **evidence from the sources** and **your own knowledge** to reach a balanced conclusion. **5**

[END OF CONTEXT IA]

UNIT I—CHANGING LIFE IN SCOTLAND AND BRITAIN

CONTEXT B: 1830s–1930s

SECTION A: KNOWLEDGE AND UNDERSTANDING

> The work in the mines was not as physical as it had been in 1830.

1. Describe the improvements in coal mining brought about by new technology up to 1930. **4**

> In most towns business people put up cheap housing to rent to working people.

2. Explain why there was so much poor housing in towns and cities in the nineteenth century. **4**

SECTION B: ENQUIRY SKILLS

The issue for investigating is:

> The actions of Suffragettes harmed the cause of votes for women.

Study the sources carefully and answer the questions which follow.
You should use your own knowledge where appropriate.

Source A is part of a speech made by Dr Marion Gilchrist, a leading Suffragette. She was speaking in 1908 at the opening of the new WSPU headquarters in Glasgow.

Source A

> At one time I thought it a great pity that the militant Suffragettes should create rows at Westminster. Now I have been brought round to another view. Nothing has done more for the cause of female suffrage than the militant Suffragettes. They have brought the question to the attention of the public and that is more than those who have carried on quietly for 60 years have achieved.

Source B is an extract from "Social Change in Scotland" by historian, Richard Dargie, published in 1999.

Source B

> The Suffragettes believed their extreme actions would force the government to give in to their demands. However, their law-breaking seemed to strengthen the argument that women could not be trusted with the vote. The Government took a tough line and the Suffrage movement split over whether it harmed or helped the cause.

Source C is an extract from "Women's Suffrage" written by Mrs Millicent Fawcett in 1912.

Source C

> The Women's Social and Political Union had not attracted any public notice until 1905. By adopting new and startling methods they succeeded in drawing a large amount of public attention to the cause of votes for women. However, many campaigners viewed these methods with disgust. They believed that lawful, peaceful action would prove more effective in the long run as a way of converting the public and the Government to believe in women's suffrage.

3. How useful are **Sources A** and **B** for investigating whether or not the actions of Suffragettes harmed the cause of votes for women? **4**

4. What evidence is there in the sources that the Suffragettes did harm the cause of votes for women?

   What evidence is there in the sources that the Suffragettes did **not** harm the cause of votes for women? **6**

5. How true is it to say that the actions of the Suffragettes harmed the cause of votes for women?

   You must use **evidence from the sources** and **your own knowledge** to reach a balanced conclusion. **5**

[*END OF CONTEXT IB*]

UNIT I—CHANGING LIFE IN SCOTLAND AND BRITAIN

CONTEXT C: 1880s–Present Day

SECTION A: KNOWLEDGE AND UNDERSTANDING

> Throughout the 1900s there were several changes in the way ships were built.

1. Describe how new technology improved shipbuilding in the twentieth century. **4**

> The general condition of housing in the cities was slowly improving.

2. How far do you agree that the condition of housing in Scotland improved after 1945? **4**

SECTION B: ENQUIRY SKILLS

The issue for investigating is:

> The actions of Suffragettes harmed the cause of votes for women.

Study the sources carefully and answer the questions which follow.
You should use your own knowledge where appropriate.

Source A is part of a speech made by Dr Marion Gilchrist, a leading Suffragette. She was speaking in 1908 at the opening of the new WSPU headquarters in Glasgow.

Source A

> At one time I thought it a great pity that the militant Suffragettes should create rows at Westminster. Now I have been brought round to another view. Nothing has done more for the cause of female suffrage than the militant Suffragettes. They have brought the question to the attention of the public and that is more than those who have carried on quietly for 60 years have achieved.

Source B is an extract from "Social Change in Scotland" by historian, Richard Dargie, published in 1999.

Source B

> The Suffragettes believed their extreme actions would force the government to give in to their demands. However, their law-breaking seemed to strengthen the argument that women could not be trusted with the vote. The Government took a tough line and the Suffrage movement split over whether it harmed or helped the cause.

Source C is an extract from "Women's Suffrage" written by Mrs Millicent Fawcett in 1912.

Source C

> The Women's Social and Political Union had not attracted any public notice until 1905. By adopting new and startling methods they succeeded in drawing a large amount of public attention to the cause of votes for women. However, many campaigners viewed these methods with disgust. They believed that lawful, peaceful action would prove more effective in the long run as a way of converting the public and the Government to believe in women's suffrage.

Marks

3. How useful are **Sources A** and **B** for investigating whether or not the actions of Suffragettes harmed the cause of votes for women? **4**

4. What evidence is there in the sources that the Suffragettes did harm the cause of votes for women?

   What evidence is there in the sources that the Suffragettes did **not** harm the cause of votes for women? **6**

5. How true is it to say that the actions of the Suffragettes harmed the cause of votes for women?

   You must use **evidence from the sources** and **your own knowledge** to reach a balanced conclusion. **5**

[END OF CONTEXT IC]

UNIT II—INTERNATIONAL COOPERATION AND CONFLICT

CONTEXT A: 1790s–1820s

SECTION A: KNOWLEDGE AND UNDERSTANDING

> In the autumn of 1792 other events occurred which hastened the war.

(Note: for this answer you should write a short essay of several paragraphs.)

1. How important in causing the outbreak of war between France and other European states between 1792 and 1793 was

   EITHER

   (a) the fear of Revolution? **8**

   OR

   (b) aggressive French foreign policy? **8**

SECTION B: ENQUIRY SKILLS

The following sources are about British attitudes to the French Revolution.

**Study the sources carefully and answer the questions which follow.
You should use your own knowledge where appropriate.**

Source A is part of a report which appeared in a Scottish newspaper, the Caledonian Mercury, in September 1790.

Source A

> In France, the triumph of liberty and reason over despotism is an interesting event. That some disturbances and even acts of violence should accompany this great Revolution is in no way surprising; that these have not been more numerous is surprising to every politician. Our hopes in Britain are that the French example will be universally followed, and that the flame they have kindled will consume the remains of despotism in Europe.

2. Discuss the attitude of the author in **Source A** to the French Revolution. **4**

Source B is from "British Social and Economic History" by historian, C. P. Hill.

Source B

> The French Revolution of 1789 had at first been universally welcomed by many Englishmen of all classes who saw it as a great move towards freedom. This attitude soon changed. The growth of violence and the intention of the leaders of the Revolution to thrust their ideas upon other people swung the ruling classes in Britain against the Revolution.

3. How fully do **Sources A** and **B** show the reaction in Britain towards events in France? You must use **your own knowledge** and give reasons for your answer.   **5**

[END OF CONTEXT IIA]

UNIT II—INTERNATIONAL COOPERATION AND CONFLICT

CONTEXT B: 1890s–1920s

SECTION A: KNOWLEDGE AND UNDERSTANDING

Alliances and military and naval rivalry hastened the outbreak of war in 1914.

(Note: for this answer you should write a short essay of several paragraphs.)

1. How important as a cause of the First World War was

   EITHER

   (a) the Alliance System? **8**

   OR

   (b) the Naval Arms Race? **8**

SECTION B: ENQUIRY SKILLS

The following sources are about British attitudes to the use of poison gas in the First World War.

**Study the sources carefully and answer the questions which follow.
You should use your own knowledge where appropriate.**

In **Source A** Sir Arthur Conan Doyle writes about a gas attack in 1915.

Source A

> Poison gas was a dreadful weapon which most cruelly affected the victim. The Germans won ground using the methods of the mass murderer. Their great army became in a single day an object of tremendous horror and great contempt.

2. Discuss the attitude of the author of **Source A** towards the use of poison gas. **4**

In **Source B** a British soldier writes about the aftermath of a gas attack.

Source B

> We have heaps of gassed soldiers. The poor things are burnt all over with great blisters and blind eyes all glued together. They speak in a merest whisper saying their throats are closing and they will choke.

3. How fully do **Sources A** and **B** describe the use of gas in the First World War?

   You must use **your own knowledge** and give reasons for your answer. 5

[END OF CONTEXT IIB]

UNIT II—INTERNATIONAL COOPERATION AND CONFLICT

CONTEXT C: 1930s–1960s

SECTION A: KNOWLEDGE AND UNDERSTANDING

> During the 1930s there was a growing danger of a new world war.

(**Note: for this answer you should write a short essay of several paragraphs.**)

1. How important as a cause of the Second World War was

   EITHER

   (a) German rearmament in the 1930s?   8

   OR

   (b) Hitler's actions against Czechoslovakia, 1938–1939?   8

SECTION B: ENQUIRY SKILLS

The following sources reflect different attitudes to the Cuban missile crisis of 1962.

**Study the sources carefully and answer the questions which follow.
You should use your own knowledge where appropriate.**

Source A is part of a broadcast by US President J. F. Kennedy on 22 October, 1962.

Source A

> These new Soviet missile sites on Cuba include medium-range ballistic missiles which are capable of striking Washington DC or any other city in the south eastern part of the United States. Other sites not yet finished are designed for intermediate-range ballistic missiles capable of striking most of the major cities in the Western Hemisphere.

2. How fully does **Source A** explain the US view of the Cuban missile crisis?

   You must use **your own knowledge** and give reasons for your answer.   5

Marks

Source B is part of a message from the Russian leader, N. Khrushchev, to President Kennedy on 27 October, 1962.

Source B

> You want to make your country safe. This is understandable, but Cuba too wants the same thing. All countries want to make themselves safe. But how are we, the Soviet Union, to assess your actions when you have surrounded the Soviet Union with military bases. This is no secret. Your rockets are situated in Turkey. You are worried about Cuba because it is only 90 miles from America. But Turkey is right next to us.

3. Discuss the attitude of the author of **Source B** towards America.   **4**

[END OF CONTEXT IIC]

UNIT III—PEOPLE AND POWER

CONTEXT A: USA 1850–1880

SECTION A: KNOWLEDGE AND UNDERSTANDING

> Americans believed it was their "Manifest Destiny" to fill the continent with white settlers.

1. Describe some of the problems faced by the native Americans ("Indians") as a result of white westward expansion. **4**

> Life for everyone in the Reconstruction South was difficult.

2. Explain why there was widespread discontent in the South after the Civil War. **4**

SECTION B: ENQUIRY SKILLS

The following sources relate to the election of Lincoln and the new Republican government.

**Study the sources carefully and answer the questions which follow.
You should use your own knowledge where appropriate.**

Source A is a poster published by the Republican party in 1860.

Source A

> **THE UNION**
> **IT MUST AND SHALL BE PRESERVED**
>
> Rally round the flag, boys
> Rally once again!!!
>
> **FOR PRESIDENT OF THE UNITED STATES**
>
> **ABRAHAM LINCOLN**
>
> who says:
>
> "My main object is to save the Union and not either to save or destroy slavery. What I do about slavery and the colored race I do because I believe it helps to save the Union."

Marks

3. How useful is **Source A** as evidence of Lincoln's policies if elected as President?   4

Source B is taken from South Carolina's "Declaration of Secession" published in December, 1860.

Source B

> A line has been drawn across the Union. All the states North of that line have been united in the election of a President who is against slavery. The Republican Party will become the government and the South shall be excluded. A war will be waged against slavery until slavery shall cease throughout the United States. With Lincoln as President, the equal rights of the states will be lost. The slaveholding states will no longer have the power of self government. The American Government will have become their enemy.

4. Discuss the views expressed in **Source B** about the effects of Lincoln's election.   4

5. To what extent does **Source B** disagree with **Source A** about Lincoln's policies?   4

[END OF CONTEXT IIIA]

UNIT III—PEOPLE AND POWER

CONTEXT B: INDIA 1917–1947

SECTION A: KNOWLEDGE AND UNDERSTANDING

> Gandhi said, "It is the old method of divide and rule. We divide and you rule."

1. Describe some of the divisions amongst Indian people living under British rule. **4**

> In August 1942, Congress declared a "Quit India" campaign.

2. Explain why the Congress Party gained support from the Indian population. **4**

SECTION B: ENQUIRY SKILLS

The following sources give evidence about Gandhi's opposition to British rule.

**Study the sources carefully and answer the questions which follow.
You should use your own knowledge where appropriate.**

Source A is a British cartoon which appeared on the day that Gandhi's Salt March began in March, 1930.

Source A

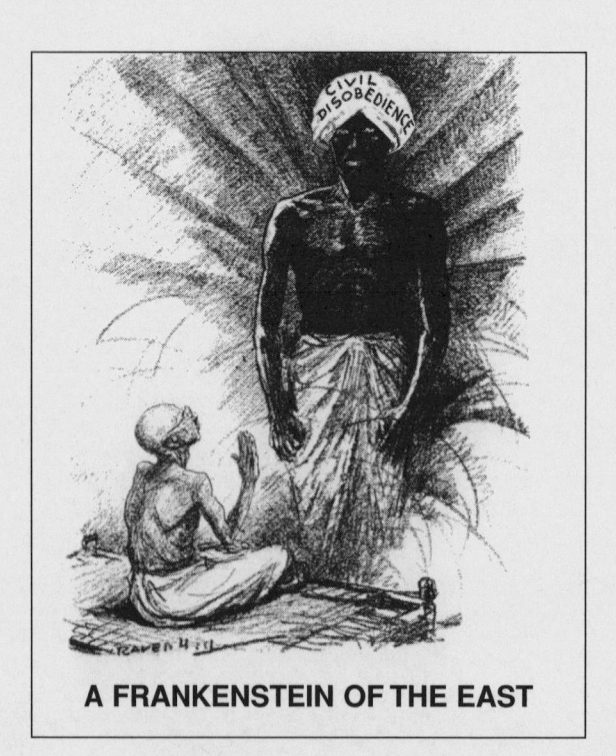

A FRANKENSTEIN OF THE EAST

GANDHI: "Remember—no violence; just disobedience"
INDIAN GENIE: "And what if I disobey you?"

Marks

3. How useful is **Source A** as evidence of British attitudes towards Gandhi's non-violent tactics? 4

Source B is a letter from Gandhi to the British Viceroy in March, 1930.

Source B

> While I think British rule of India is a curse, I do not intend harm to a single British person. Nothing but organised non-violence can check the organised violence of the British government. This non-violence will be expressed through civil disobedience. My ambition is to convert the British people and make them see the wrong they have done to India. Civil disobedience will be peaceful and with it we will combat evils such as the salt tax. This letter is not intended as a threat, but I feel it is my duty as a civil resister to send it to you.

4. Compare the views about civil disobedience in **Sources A** and **B**. 4

5. Discuss Gandhi's attitude towards British rule in India as shown in **Source B**. 4

[END OF CONTEXT IIIB]

UNIT III—PEOPLE AND POWER

CONTEXT C: RUSSIA 1914–1941

SECTION A: KNOWLEDGE AND UNDERSTANDING

> Although the peasants had been freed from serfdom, things had not improved for most of them.

1. Describe some of the hardships faced by Russian peasants before 1917. **4**

> Within six months Lenin was urging that the time was right for the Bolsheviks to seize power.

2. Explain why, by October 1917, Lenin thought the time was right for the Bolsheviks to seize power. **4**

SECTION B: ENQUIRY SKILLS

The following sources relate to collectivisation in Russia between 1927 and 1934.

**Study the sources carefully and answer the questions which follow.
You should use your own knowledge where appropriate.**

Source A is from Stalin's speech to the Party Congress in 1927.

Source A

> The way to improve agriculture is to turn the small and scattered peasant farms into large united farms based on the common cultivation of the land. The way ahead is to unite the small peasant farms gradually but surely, not by pressure but by example and persuasion, into large farms based on common, cooperative collective cultivation of the land. There is no other way to improve.

3. Discuss Stalin's attitude towards agricultural change in Russia. **4**

Marks

Source B is a Soviet government photograph from the 1930s showing a Communist Party worker talking to peasants about collectivisation.

Source B

4. How useful is **Source B** as evidence of how collectivisation was achieved in Russia? **4**

Source C is from "Dreams, Plans and Nightmares" by Tony Howarth.

Source C

> Some peasants in the villages, especially the poorer ones, were in favour of collectivisation. So were the local rural soviets; and 25 000 trusted party men from the cities were sent to encourage collectivisation. They also threatened and bullied and where peasants resisted, the security police turned up with armed men and machine guns.

5. To what extent do **Sources B** and **C** agree about the methods used to bring about collectivisation? **4**

[END OF CONTEXT IIIC]

Marks

UNIT III—PEOPLE AND POWER

CONTEXT D: GERMANY 1918–1939

SECTION A: KNOWLEDGE AND UNDERSTANDING

> When the news of the Treaty reached the German people the reaction was one of predictable anger.

1. Describe some of the reasons for German anger over the Treaty of Versailles. **4**

> Historians still debate why so many people supported the Nazi state.

2. Explain why many Germans supported the Nazis between 1933 and 1939. **4**

SECTION B: ENQUIRY SKILLS

The following sources give evidence about the treatment of the Jews in Germany.

**Study the sources carefully and answer the questions which follow.
You should use your own knowledge where appropriate.**

Source A shows Jewish children being made a fool of at school in 1935. The wording on the blackboard says "The Jews are our greatest enemy. Beware of the Jews."

Source A

3. How useful is **Source A** as evidence of the treatment of Jewish children in Nazi Germany? **4**

Source B is an extract from the memoirs of a Jewish woman, Alice Solomon. It describes the treatment of a Jewish child at school in 1935.

Source B

> One day she came home humiliated. "It was not so nice today", she said. What had happened? The teacher had placed the Aryan children to one side of the classroom, and the non-Aryans to the other. Then the teacher told the Aryans to study the appearance of the others and to point out the marks of their Jewish race. They stood separated as if by a gulf. Children who had played together as friends the day before were now enemies.

4. To what extent do **Sources A** and **B** agree about the treatment of Jewish children at school in Nazi Germany? **4**

In **Source C** a Jew from Munich describes the treatment he received on Crystal Night in November 1938.

Source C

> The mood among the Christian population in Munich is wholly opposed to the action against the Jewish population. I personally encountered much sympathy and compassion from all sides. Aryan people from the area offered to shelter my family for the night. Despite the harsh ban on sales to Jews, grocers asked Jews whether they needed anything. Bakers delivered bread to Jewish families, ignoring the ban.

5. Discuss the attitudes of the people in Munich towards the Jews, as shown in **Source C**. **4**

[END OF CONTEXT IIID]

[END OF QUESTION PAPER]

[BLANK PAGE]

2002 CREDIT

1540/403

NATIONAL
QUALIFICATIONS
2002

MONDAY, 20 MAY
1.00 PM – 2.45 PM

HISTORY
STANDARD GRADE
Credit Level

Answer questions from Unit I **and** Unit II **and** Unit III.

Choose only **one** Context from each Unit and answer Sections A **and** B. The Contexts chosen should be those you have studied.

The Contexts in each Unit are:

Unit I— Changing Life in Scotland and Britain
 Context A: 1750s–1850s .... Pages 2–3
 Context B: 1830s–1930s .... Pages 4–5
 Context C: 1880s–Present Day .... Pages 6–7

Unit II— International Cooperation and Conflict
 Context A: 1790s–1820s .... Pages 8–9
 Context B: 1890s–1920s .... Pages 10–11
 Context C: 1930s–1960s ....Pages 12–13

Unit III— People and Power
 Context A: USA 1850–1880.......................... Pages 14–15
 Context B: India 1917–1947 .... Pages 16–17
 Context C: Russia 1914–1941...................... Pages 18–19
 Context D: Germany 1918–1939 .... Pages 20–21

Number the questions as shown in the question paper.

Some sources have been adapted or translated.

UNIT I—CHANGING LIFE IN SCOTLAND AND BRITAIN

CONTEXT A: 1750s–1850s

SECTION A: KNOWLEDGE AND UNDERSTANDING

> The life of the ordinary person was subject to many dangers over which he had little or no control.

(Note: for this answer you should write a short essay of several paragraphs.)

1. Explain fully the reasons why people living in nineteenth-century Scotland faced difficulties due to

EITHER

(a) problems with housing. **8**

OR

(b) problems with health. **8**

SECTION B: ENQUIRY SKILLS

The issue for investigating is:

> In the early nineteenth century, Scottish textile mills provided acceptable working conditions for the work force.

Study the sources carefully and answer the questions which follow.
You should use your own knowledge where appropriate.

Source A is from the Report of Commissioners on the Employment of Children in Factories, 1833.

Source A

> The rooms in Deanston Mill (in Stirlingshire) are well ventilated and have the machinery well fenced. The windows are constructed so that the whole of the upper part of each window may be let down. There are rooms for the workers to dress and undress in, and piped water to each storey. Sewering arrangements are adopted throughout.

Marks

Source B is from "Expansion, Trade and Industry" by historian C. Culpin, written in 1993.

Source B

> It must have been hard for people used to working on their own at home, at their own speed, to fit into factory work. The powered machines went on, hour after hour, and workers had to keep up with them. Owners of the first factories had strict rules to enforce discipline. Workers had to do as they were told or lose their jobs. There were no safety laws and no protective guards on dangerous machines.

Source C is from an official investigation into working conditions in textile mills in 1833.

Source C

> Large, recently built mills are, without exception, more spacious. The buildings are better drained and more effective methods are used to maintain a moderate temperature. Older, smaller mills have no accommodation for washing or dressing and no machinery for carrying off dust. Some of the rooms are so low that it is scarcely possible to stand upright in the centre of the room.

2. How useful are **Sources A** and **B** for investigating working conditions in Scottish textile mills in the nineteenth century? **4**

3. What evidence is there in the sources to support the view that the Scottish textile industry in the nineteenth century provided good working conditions?

   What evidence in the sources suggests that the Scottish textile industry in the nineteenth century did **not** provide good working conditions? **6**

4. How true is it to say that in the early nineteenth century the Scottish textile mills provided acceptable working conditions for the work force?

   You must use **evidence from the sources** and **your own knowledge** to reach a balanced conclusion. **5**

[END OF CONTEXT IA]

UNIT I—CHANGING LIFE IN SCOTLAND AND BRITAIN

CONTEXT B: 1830s–1930s

SECTION A: KNOWLEDGE AND UNDERSTANDING

> This was a period of significant improvement in the everyday life of the British people.

(Note: for this answer you should write a short essay of several paragraphs.)

1. Explain fully the reasons why people's lives got better between 1830 and 1930 as a result of

   EITHER

   (a) improvements in health. **8**

   OR

   (b) improvements in housing. **8**

SECTION B: ENQUIRY SKILLS

The issue for investigating is:

> By the 1930s working conditions had greatly improved in Scottish coal mines.

Study the sources carefully and answer the questions which follow.
You should use your own knowledge where appropriate.

Source A is from "Britain Transformed" written in 1987 by the historian, Malcolm Falkus.

Source A

> In the later nineteenth century steam driven fans were installed to circulate air in mines. Underground explosions were considerably lessened by the invention of the Davy Safety Lamp. Strong, wire rope became more widely used in all pits. Increasingly, collieries used steam engines for their winding gear. Aspects of safety were also improved by Acts of Parliament.

Marks

Source B was written in 1869 by David Bremner after his visit to Arniston Colliery in Midlothian.

Source B

> The miners enter the pit between 5 and 6 o'clock in the morning. They are in constant danger of a violent death or of injury. The winding gear may give way and there are the dangers of being suffocated by foul air or of being scorched to death by the ignition of fire damp (methane). In 1865 in Scotland 12 034 638 tons of coal were raised and 77 lives lost.

Source C is from a history textbook and is about working conditions in mines in the 1930s.

Source C

> The dangers of roof falls and cage accidents were still present, though rarer, and fewer lives were lost than in the past. However, new machinery created more dust and more lung disease. Safety clothing was only being introduced in the 1930s. Government legislation resulted in improvements and the miners continued to press for better pay and conditions.

2. How useful are **Sources A** and **B** for investigating improved working conditions in Scottish coal mines in the nineteenth century? **4**

3. What evidence is there in the sources that working conditions in Scottish coal mines were improving?

   What evidence in the sources suggests that working conditions in Scottish coal mines had **not** greatly improved? **6**

4. To what extent did working conditions greatly improve in Scottish coal mines by the 1930s?

   You must use **evidence from the sources** and **your own knowledge** to reach a balanced conclusion. **5**

[END OF CONTEXT IB]

UNIT I—CHANGING LIFE IN SCOTLAND AND BRITAIN

CONTEXT C: 1880s–Present Day

SECTION A: KNOWLEDGE AND UNDERSTANDING

> In most parts of Scotland the standards of health and housing greatly improved during the twentieth century.

(Note: for this answer you should write a short essay of several paragraphs.)

1. Explain fully the reasons why people's lives got better in twentieth-century Scotland as a result of

EITHER

(a) improvements in health.   **8**

OR

(b) improvements in housing.   **8**

SECTION B: ENQUIRY SKILLS

The issue for investigating is:

> Employment opportunities for women were greatly changed by the First World War.

Study the sources carefully and answer the questions which follow.
You should use your own knowledge where appropriate.

Source A is an extract from "The Scottish Nation 1700–2000" by Professor T. M. Devine.

Source A

> Male trade unionists strongly supported the idea of "separate spheres" for men and women in which the woman's place was very much in the home. This belief was threatened by the First World War. Women flooded into the munitions factories, engineering workshops and numerous other areas of the economy formerly dominated by men. However, the old ideas about women were very strong and it is no longer possible to speak about the Great War as a turning point in the emancipation of working women.

Marks

Source B was published in the Glasgow Evening Citizen newspaper in April, 1916.

Source B

> When the history of the war is written, the part played by women will be one of its finest chapters. From every class they have come forward to help their country: as nurses, as workers and in the thousand and one occupations in town and country that were previously filled by men.

Source C is from "The Cause" by E. R. Strachey, written in 1928.

Source C

> After the war, thousands of women workers were dismissed and could find no work to do. It was terribly hard on women. Everyone assumed they would go quietly back to their homes but this was impossible. War deaths had enormously increased the number of surplus women so that one in three had to be self-supporting. The tone of the press changed and the very same women who had been heroines were now parasites.

2. How useful are **Sources A** and **B** for investigating the effects of the First World War on women's employment opportunities? **4**

3. What evidence is there in the sources to support the view that the First World War greatly changed employment opportunities for women?

   What evidence is there in the sources to support the view that the First World War did **not** greatly change employment opportunities for women? **6**

4. To what extent did the First World War greatly change employment opportunities for women?

   You must use **evidence from the sources** and **your own knowledge** to reach a balanced conclusion. **5**

[END OF CONTEXT IC]

UNIT II—INTERNATIONAL COOPERATION AND CONFLICT

CONTEXT A: 1790s–1820s

SECTION A: KNOWLEDGE AND UNDERSTANDING

> As the French Revolution daily grew more violent, so the danger of war increased.

1. How important was the fear of revolution in causing the war between Britain and France? **4**

> There was considerable discontent in the navy and this was to show itself in the mutinies of 1797.

2. Describe the hardships faced by sailors in the navy during the Wars with France. **5**

SECTION B: ENQUIRY SKILLS

The following sources are about the Congress of Vienna in 1815.

**Study the sources carefully and answer the questions which follow.
You should use your own knowledge where appropriate.**

Source A is from the writings of the nineteenth-century Italian politician, Cavour.

Source A

> The Congress of Vienna built a Europe without moral or just foundations. It relied upon no principle, neither rights of legal rulers, nor national interests, nor the will of the people. It took no account of geographical conditions or of general interests and acted only by right of the strongest.

3. Discuss the attitude of Cavour to the settlement reached at the Congress of Vienna. **4**

Marks

In **Source B**, the historians D. Richards and J. W. Hunt give their view of the Congress of Vienna.

Source B

> The treaties completely ignored the spirit of nationality which had proved so powerful in defeating Napoleon. Countries and peoples were moved about regardless of their wishes and feelings. But, however great its faults, the settlement showed some wisdom. The chief British representative, Lord Castlereagh, determined that France should not be victimised for the faults of Napoleon.

4. To what extent do the authors of **Source B** agree with Cavour in **Source A**? 5

[END OF CONTEXT IIA]

Marks

UNIT II—INTERNATIONAL COOPERATION AND CONFLICT

CONTEXT B: 1890s–1920s

SECTION A: KNOWLEDGE AND UNDERSTANDING

> By 1914 Britain and Germany stared menacingly at each other across the North Sea.

1. How important a factor was naval rivalry in causing tension before 1914? 4

> By early 1916 trench lines were well established on the Western Front.

2. Describe what trench life was like for front line soldiers on the Western Front. 5

SECTION B: ENQUIRY SKILLS

The following sources are about the Treaty of Versailles.

**Study the sources carefully and answer the questions which follow.
You should use your own knowledge where appropriate.**

Source A was written by Sir Philip Gibbs who was a British representative at the peace conference.

Source A

> It was a peace of vengeance and consequently was very unfair. The economic terms of the Treaty were mad. Germany had to pay for all the damage caused during the war. The impossibility of getting all this money from a defeated country was obvious even to the most ignorant schoolboy.

3. Discuss the attitude of Sir Philip Gibbs towards the Treaty of Versailles. 4

Marks

Source B is part of a speech by Lloyd George in July 1919.

Source B

> The last time I spoke about the Treaty I called it a "stern but just treaty". I stick to that description. The terms are in many respects terrible terms to impose upon a country. Germany's war debt is more than doubled in order to pay reparations. However, in so far as territories have been taken away from Germany, it is a restoration—they are all territories that ought not to belong to Germany.

4. How far do **Sources A** and **B** disagree about the Treaty of Versailles? 5

[END OF CONTEXT IIB]

UNIT II—INTERNATIONAL COOPERATION AND CONFLICT

CONTEXT C: 1930s–1960s

SECTION A: KNOWLEDGE AND UNDERSTANDING

> Hitler had his eye on Czechoslovakia, especially the Sudetenland.

1. How important was the Czech crisis of 1938 as a cause of increasing tension before the Second World War? **4**

> Government wartime controls affected almost every aspect of life in Britain.

2. Describe the hardships of everyday life for civilians in Britain during the Second World War. **5**

SECTION B: ENQUIRY SKILLS

The following sources are about the changing role of Britain and its Empire.

**Study the sources carefully and answer the questions which follow.
You should use your own knowledge where appropriate.**

Source A is from the autobiography of Clement Attlee, British Prime Minister from 1945–1951.

Source A

> Our policy was to give full self-government to our former colonies. Britain is now the heart of a growing Commonwealth. This policy met with general approval except from a limited number of people, including Churchill, who regarded it as a betrayal of our imperial heritage. In fact, we have gained immensely in friendship from our policy. An attempt to maintain old colonialism would have aided communism.

3. Discuss the attitude of Clement Attlee about Britain's changing policy towards its former colonies. **4**

In **Source B** a modern historian discusses Britain's changing influence after 1945.

Source B

> In 1945 the British people still thought of their country as a great imperial power but the British were breaking up their once world-wide Empire. In a few places there was fighting but more often power was handed over peacefully. Only a few regretted this, believing that the Empire had made Britain great. Britain tried to keep on friendly terms with its old colonies through the Commonwealth, the group of independent nations who had once been part of the British Empire.

4. To what extent do **Sources A** and **B** agree about Britain's changing influence after 1945?

   5

[END OF CONTEXT IIC]

UNIT III—PEOPLE AND POWER

CONTEXT A: USA 1850–1880

SECTION A: KNOWLEDGE AND UNDERSTANDING

> When war broke out in 1861 many Northerners were firmly against slavery.

1. Explain the reasons why many people in the North were against slavery.

> After the Civil War was over the government improved the position of the freed slaves.

2. In what ways did the US government improve the conditions of the freed slaves after 1865?

SECTION B: ENQUIRY SKILLS

The following sources are about Westward expansion.

**Study the sources carefully and answer the questions which follow.
You should use your own knowledge where appropriate.**

Source A was painted by Francis Palmer in 1866. It is called "Rocky Mountains—Emigrants Crossing the Plains".

Source A

3. How useful is **Source A** as evidence of how white settlers travelled west?

In **Source B** a native American ("Indian") discusses the white settlers' attitude to land ownership.

Source B

> Why do these "People Greedily Grasping for Land" want more acres than they need to grow food on? Why do they build houses that will outlast their occupants? Why does the white man insist that land he has bought becomes his exclusively and for all time? Sell a country? Why not sell the air, the clouds and the great sea?

4. Discuss the attitude of the native American ("Indian") towards land ownership shown in **Source B**. **4**

Source C is from "The American West, 1840–1895" by R. A. Rees and S. J. Styles.

Source C

> White American Settlers believed that they were not simply looking for new and fertile farmland, they were putting the American dream into action. They were beginning the final wave of migration which would end with the whole of America being lived in by white Americans. They believed that civilisation would be brought to the wilderness.

5. How fully does the evidence given in **Source C** explain the reasons for settlers going west?

   You must use **evidence from the source** and **your own knowledge** and give reasons for your answer. **4**

[*END OF CONTEXT IIIA*]

UNIT III—PEOPLE AND POWER

CONTEXT B: INDIA 1917–1947

SECTION A: KNOWLEDGE AND UNDERSTANDING

> Lord Curzon, Viceroy of India, sincerely believed in British superiority in all things.

1. Explain in what ways many Indians were increasingly discontented with British rule after 1917.   **3**

> Gandhi's tactics have had far reaching consequences outside India.

2. Describe Gandhi's tactics in resisting British power.   **4**

SECTION B: ENQUIRY SKILLS

The following sources are about Indian Independence and Partition.

**Study the sources carefully and answer the questions which follow.
You should use your own knowledge where appropriate.**

Source A is a press photograph which appeared in British newspapers on August 16th, 1947.

Source A

NEW DELHI: INDEPENDENCE DAY
HAPPY CROWDS MOB LORD AND LADY MOUNTBATTEN

Marks

3. How useful is **Source A** as evidence of attitudes in India towards Independence? 4

Source B is from a speech given by Winston Churchill in September 1947.

Source B

> The fearful massacres which are occurring in India are no surprise to me. This is just the beginning of the horrors and butcheries which will be carried out. The peoples of India are gifted with the capacities for the highest culture and they had for generations dwelt side by side in general peace under the tolerant and impartial rule of the British Crown and Parliament. Now things will be different.

4. Discuss Winston Churchill's views about the difficulties following India's Independence. 4

Source C is from "The Long Afternoon" by William Golant.

Source C

> In the past, the two separate communities had lived uneasily together. Even under British rule the two religions had separate education and languages which contributed to an aggressive attitude toward each other's community. In some areas such as Bengal and the Punjab the majority of the population were Muslims.

5. How fully does **Source C** explain the difficulties faced by an independent India?

   You must use **evidence from the source** and **your own knowledge** and give reasons for your answer. 4

[END OF CONTEXT IIIB]

Marks

UNIT III—PEOPLE AND POWER

CONTEXT C: RUSSIA 1914–1941

SECTION A: KNOWLEDGE AND UNDERSTANDING

> "There was evidence of widespread discontent with the Tsar's government by the end of 1916."

1. Why were so many Russians discontented with the Tsar's government by late 1916? **3**

> Lenin was convinced that the time was right to take power from the Provisional Government.

2. Describe the seizure of power by the Bolsheviks in October 1917. **4**

SECTION B: ENQUIRY SKILLS

The following sources are about the Provisional Government.

**Study the sources carefully and answer the questions which follow.
You should use your own knowledge where appropriate.**

Source A is from a speech by Lenin in April 1917.

Source A

> Do not believe the promises of the Provisional Government. They are deceiving you and the whole Russian people. The people need peace; the people need bread; the people need land. And they give you war, hunger, no bread and leave the landlords still on the land. We must fight for the social revolution.

3. Discuss Lenin's views about the Provisional Government. **4**

Source B is a photograph from 1917 showing wounded soldiers demonstrating. The banner says "Continue the War until Victory is Complete".

Source B

4. How useful is **Source B** as evidence about attitudes in Russia towards the Provisional Government? 4

Source C is from "Lenin and the Russian Revolution" by Donald W. Mack.

Source C

> The Provisional Government was unable to improve matters, and the workers began to try to get control of the factories in which they worked. Some argued that Russia should be governed by the Soviets. This was what the Bolsheviks were saying so they found allies in the workers who were prepared to overthrow the Provisional Government.

5. How fully does **Source C** explain why the Provisional Government fell from power in October, 1917?

    You must use **evidence from the source** and **your own knowledge** and give reasons for your answer. 4

[*END OF CONTEXT IIIC*]

UNIT III—PEOPLE AND POWER

CONTEXT D: GERMANY 1918–1939

SECTION A: KNOWLEDGE AND UNDERSTANDING

> The Weimar Government in Germany was unpopular in the years following the Versailles Settlement.

1. Explain why the Weimar Government was unpopular with many Germans in the early 1920s.   **3**

> By 1934 Hitler was the Fuhrer with complete control over the German people.

2. Describe the ways in which Hitler gained total power in Germany.   **4**

SECTION B: ENQUIRY SKILLS

The following sources are about attitudes to the Nazis.

**Study the sources carefully and answer the questions which follow.
You should use your own knowledge where appropriate.**

Source A is an extract from the diary of Count Harry Kessler written after an election in 1932.

Source A

> A black day for Germany. The Nazis have increased their number of seats almost tenfold. They have become the second largest party in the Reichstag. The impression created abroad must be disastrous. The impact on foreign and financial affairs is likely to be very damaging. We face a national crisis. This can only be overcome if all those who accept or at least tolerate the Republic stand firmly together.

3. Discuss the attitude of Count Kessler towards the Nazis.   **4**

Source B is a Nazi poster from 1933. The German words say "Our last hope: HITLER".

Source B

[Nazi poster showing a crowd of grim-faced people with the German text "Unsere letzte Hoffnung:" at the top and "HITLER" at the bottom.]

4. How useful is **Source B** as evidence of the tactics used by the Nazis to gain support? **4**

In **Source C** a modern historian describes the problems faced by Germans who opposed the Nazis.

Source C

> The resistance movement never enjoyed much support among the masses of the working class. It was a movement of officers without soldiers: a large and uncoordinated collection of intellectuals, civil servants, diplomats and the military. Each group was rarely informed about what the other groups were doing.

5. How fully does the evidence in **Source C** explain why it was difficult to oppose the Nazis?

   You must use **evidence from the source** and **your own knowledge** and give reasons for your answer. **4**

[END OF CONTEXT IIID]

[END OF QUESTION PAPER]

[BLANK PAGE]

2003 CREDIT

1540/403

NATIONAL
QUALIFICATIONS
2003

MONDAY, 12 MAY
1.00 PM – 2.45 PM

HISTORY
STANDARD GRADE
Credit Level

Answer questions from Unit I **and** Unit II **and** Unit III.

Choose only **one** Context from each Unit and answer Sections A **and** B. The Contexts chosen should be those you have studied.

The Contexts in each Unit are:

   Unit I— Changing Life in Scotland and Britain
      Context A: 1750s–1850s .... Pages 2–3
      Context B: 1830s–1930s .... Pages 4–5
      Context C: 1880s–Present Day .... Pages 6–7

   Unit II— International Cooperation and Conflict
      Context A: 1790s–1820s .... Pages 8–9
      Context B: 1890s–1920s .... Pages 10–11
      Context C: 1930s–1960s .... Pages 12–13

   Unit III— People and Power
      Context A: USA 1850–1880.......................... Pages 14–15
      Context B: India 1917–1947 .... Pages 16–17
      Context C: Russia 1914–1941 .... Pages 18–19
      Context D: Germany 1918–1939 .... Pages 20–21

Number the questions as shown in the question paper.

Some sources have been adapted or translated.

UNIT I—CHANGING LIFE IN SCOTLAND AND BRITAIN

CONTEXT A: 1750s–1850s

SECTION A: KNOWLEDGE AND UNDERSTANDING

> After 1750 many Scottish landowners began to improve the old run rig system of farming.

1. Explain why farming methods improved after 1750. **5**

> Before 1832 the number of people who could vote in Scotland was very restricted.

2. Describe the improvements to democracy in Scotland made by the 1832 Reform Act. **4**

SECTION B: ENQUIRY SKILLS

The issue for investigating is:

> Better medical knowledge was the main cause of population growth in Scotland between 1750 and 1850.

Study the sources carefully and answer the questions which follow.
You should use your own knowledge where appropriate.

Source A is from "Changing Life in Scotland and Britain" by historians R. Cameron, C. Henderson and C. Robertson, published in 1997.

Source A

> Medical knowledge made significant progress during the 19th century. Vaccinating people against smallpox had been discovered by Edward Jenner in 1796. Deaths from smallpox fell from about 3000 per million in 1800 to 500 per million in 1840. James Simpson perfected the use of chloroform as the first reasonably safe and effective anaesthetic for childbirth and surgery. These developments were a factor in the falling death rate.

Source B is taken from the New Statistical Account for Dundee, 1833.

Source B

> The cause of this extraordinary increase in population is due to the great growth of the linen trade which has produced so many spinning mills. By giving employment to thousands it has encouraged early marriages (and more children), as well as bringing families from other parts of Scotland and from Ireland.

Source C is from "The New Penguin History of Scotland" published in 2001.

Source C

> Between 1750 and 1850 the population of Scotland experienced unprecedented growth. From 1750 annual growth in numbers jumped to 1·2 per cent. Excellent by contemporary standards though Scottish medicine was, it contributed little to the fading away of epidemic diseases. Bubonic plague just ceased to happen while better quarantine procedures prevented its reintroduction. Improved incomes by 1800 may have enhanced diet.

3. How useful are **Sources A** and **B** for investigating the causes of population rise in Scotland between 1750 and 1850? **4**

Look at Sources A, B and C.

4. What evidence is there in the sources to support the view that better medical knowledge caused population growth in Scotland?

    What evidence is there in the sources to suggest that there were other reasons for population growth in Scotland? **6**

5. How far do you agree that better medical knowledge was the main cause of population growth in Scotland between 1750 and 1850?

    You must use **evidence from the sources** and **your own knowledge** to reach a balanced conclusion. **5**

[END OF CONTEXT IA]

UNIT I—CHANGING LIFE IN SCOTLAND AND BRITAIN

CONTEXT B: 1830s–1930s

SECTION A: KNOWLEDGE AND UNDERSTANDING

> The coming of the railways brought new opportunities to many people in Scotland.

1. Explain why many people benefitted from the coming of the railways. — 5

> It was from the leisured middle classes that the demand for votes for women first came.

2. Describe the non violent methods used by women to campaign for the vote. — 4

SECTION B: ENQUIRY SKILLS

The issue for investigating is:

> Population growth between 1830 and 1930 was largely due to medical factors.

Study the sources carefully and answer the questions which follow.
You should use your own knowledge where appropriate.

Source A is statistical evidence from the Registrar General's returns in 1884.

Source A

> The expectation of life is three years longer now than for the previous period of seventeen years ending in 1884. This increase in the length of life is probably due to the abolition of the duty on soap. It has been helped by the ending of the window tax, as well as by improvement to the water supply.

Source B is from "A Century of the Scottish People" by Professor T. C. Smout, published in 1986.

Source B

> Much of the improvement in infant mortality since 1900 might be attributed to the gradual decrease, since 1870, in the overwork, malnutrition and serious disease of girls and young women. This was assisted in the twentieth century by the introduction of medical inspection in schools and also to general improvements in medical care during and after birth itself.

Source C is from "The Scottish Nation 1700–2000" by T. M. Devine, published in 1999.

Source C

> The direct causes of mortality decline included the control and then the steady reduction of lethal diseases of childhood. This was achieved by improvement of the urban environment through the provision of cleaner water and better sewerage. The efforts of doctors, nurses and midwives were also beginning to be felt in working class communities.

3. How useful are **Sources A** and **B** for investigating the causes of population growth between 1830 and 1930? **4**

Look at Sources A, B and C.

4. What evidence is there in the sources to support the view that medical factors were a cause of population growth?

    What evidence is there in the sources to suggest that there were other reasons for population growth in Scotland? **6**

5. How far do you agree that population growth between 1830 and 1930 was largely due to medical factors?

    You must use **evidence from the sources** and **your own knowledge** to reach a balanced conclusion. **5**

[END OF CONTEXT IB]

UNIT I—CHANGING LIFE IN SCOTLAND AND BRITAIN

CONTEXT C: 1880s–Present Day

SECTION A: KNOWLEDGE AND UNDERSTANDING

> The shipyards of the Clyde were in deep trouble by the 1970s.

1. Explain why Scottish shipbuilding was in trouble by the 1970s. — **5**

> It was from the leisured middle classes that the demand for votes for women first came.

2. Describe the non violent methods used by women to campaign for the vote. — **4**

SECTION B: ENQUIRY SKILLS

The issue for investigating is:

> Better health care was the main cause of population growth between 1880 and 1980.

**Study the sources carefully and answer the questions which follow.
You should use your own knowledge where appropriate.**

Source A is from an official medical report to the Government published in 1972.

Source A

> A century ago tuberculosis was the most fatal of all diseases in Britain. It killed many children. In 1900 the death rate due to tuberculosis was 360 in every 1000 of the population. Today that figure has fallen to 10 for men and 3 for women in every 1000. Many factors have contributed to these results: better diet, earlier diagnosis through mass X-rays and the success of the B.C.G. vaccination campaign.

Source B is an extract from "A Social and Economic History of Industrial Britain" by John Robottom, published in 1986.

Source B

> Since 1948 the most obvious cause of a rising population has been the final victory against fevers which killed thousands as recently as fifty years ago. Immunisation has wiped out diphtheria and typhoid. For a time, there were growing numbers of victims of polio until it was beaten by new vaccines. Rising living standards and free medical treatment have brought about a big improvement in general health and consequent population growth.

Source C is an extract from "British Economic and Social History" by Philip Sauvain, published in 1988.

Source C

> Improvements in living standards and nursing care helped to bring the death rate down in the early years of the twentieth century. In the last thirty years, the decline of heavy industry, the introduction of effective legislation to minimise air pollution and the use of antibiotics have all helped to reduce the incidence of disease and have brought down the death rate still further.

3. How useful are **Sources A** and **B** for investigating the causes of population growth between 1880 and 1980? **4**

Look at Sources A, B and C.

4. What evidence is there in the sources to support the view that better health care was a cause of population growth between 1880 and 1980?

    What evidence is there in the sources that other factors caused population growth between 1880 and 1980? **6**

5. How far do you agree that better health care was the main cause of population growth between 1880 and 1980?

    You must use **evidence from the sources** and **your own knowledge** to reach a balanced conclusion. **5**

[END OF CONTEXT IC]

UNIT II—INTERNATIONAL COOPERATION AND CONFLICT

CONTEXT A: 1790s–1820s

SECTION A: KNOWLEDGE AND UNDERSTANDING

> In both Britain and France, the long war seriously affected the civilian population.

(Note: for this answer you should write a short essay of several paragraphs.)

1. How far do you agree that during the Napoleonic Wars the difficulty of food supply was the most important problem faced by

   EITHER

   (a) civilians in Britain? **8**

   OR

   (b) civilians in France? **8**

SECTION B: ENQUIRY SKILLS

The following sources are about George Canning and the Congress System.

Study the sources carefully and answer the questions which follow.
You should use your own knowledge where appropriate.

Source A is part of an official instruction written by George Canning, British Foreign Minister at the Congress of Verona in 1822.

Source A

> If there is a proposal to interfere by force in the present struggle in Spain, so convinced is the British Government of the danger of such interference, that you must say that Britain will not agree to participate with the other Congress powers in such interference.

2. How useful is **Source A** as evidence of Britain's attitude to the Congress System? **4**

Marks

Source B is from "Europe Since Napoleon" by David Thompson.

Source B

> At the Congress of Verona in 1822, Britain was represented by George Canning whose hostility to congresses and armed intervention into other states was even stronger than that of Castlereagh whom he had had replaced as Foreign Minister. Canning's firm resistance to intervention stopped the members of the Congress System from taking any action in Spain. Canning's complaints at Verona marked the completion of the breach between Britain and her Congress partners.

3. Discuss David Thompson's opinions of George Canning at the Congress of Verona. **4**

Source C is from a biography of George Canning.

Source C

> George Canning was recalled to the Foreign Office after Castlereagh's death. He reversed previous policy towards the Holy Alliance and refused to cooperate with other Congress partners if it meant intervening into other countries to put down revolutions. He protested about many of the decisions at the Congress of Verona but was unable to prevent French intervention in Spain.

4. How far do **Sources B** and **C** agree about George Canning at the Congress of Verona? **4**

[*END OF CONTEXT IIA*]

UNIT II—INTERNATIONAL COOPERATION AND CONFLICT

CONTEXT B: 1890s–1920s

SECTION A: KNOWLEDGE AND UNDERSTANDING

> In both Britain and Germany, the years of war took their toll on the civilian population.

(Note: for this answer you should write a short essay of several paragraphs.)

1. How far do you agree that during the First World War, the difficulty of food supply was the most important problem faced by

   EITHER

   (a) civilians in Britain? **8**

   OR

   (b) civilians in Germany? **8**

SECTION B: ENQUIRY SKILLS

The following sources are about the League of Nations.

**Study the sources carefully and answer the questions which follow.
You should use your own knowledge where appropriate.**

Source A is part of a speech made by Arthur Balfour, chief British representative at the League of Nations in 1920.

Source A

> The League of Nations is not set up to deal with a world in chaos, or with any part of the world which is in trouble. The League of Nations may give assistance but it is not, and cannot be, a complete instrument for bringing order out of chaos.

2. How useful is **Source A** as evidence of attitudes towards the League of Nations? **4**

Source B is from "The League of Nations" by historians Gibbons and Morican.

Source B

> The League, handicapped as it was by the absence of major powers, did achieve a measure of success during the Corfu crisis. The League had been designed to deal with just such a dangerous problem as this. It had acted fairly and promptly and it had condemned the violence of the Italians towards the Greeks. But it had lost the initiative. The result was that a great power had once again got away with using force against a small power.

3. Discuss the attitude of the authors of **Source B** towards the League of Nations. **4**

Source C is from "World History from 1914" by Christopher Culpin.

Source C

> The most serious blow was the refusal of the USA to become a member. The League was consequently weakened when it came to dealing with incidents such as the Corfu crisis. The League quickly discussed the matter and offered a solution. However, under pressure from the Italian dictator, Mussolini, the terms of the agreement were altered in favour of Italy. The League had been ready to act but the Great Powers acted on their own, ignoring the League. Bullying tactics had paid off.

4. How far do **Sources B** and **C** agree about the League of Nations? **4**

[*END OF CONTEXT IIB*]

UNIT II—INTERNATIONAL COOPERATION AND CONFLICT

CONTEXT C: 1930s–1960s

SECTION A: KNOWLEDGE AND UNDERSTANDING

> In both Britain and Germany, the long war took its toll on the civilian population.

(Note: for this answer you should write a short essay of several paragraphs.)

1. How far do you agree that during the Second World War, the difficulty of food supply was the most important problem faced by

EITHER

(a) civilians in Britain? **8**

OR

(b) civilians in Germany? **8**

SECTION B: ENQUIRY SKILLS

The following sources are about the Berlin Crisis of 1948.

**Study the sources carefully and answer the questions which follow.
You should use your own knowledge where appropriate.**

Source A was published by the Soviet News Agency, "Tass", in May 1948.

Source A

> All road and rail routes into Berlin are now closed. The Soviet authorities are ready to provide food and fuel for the population of the whole of Berlin, but the Western powers are depriving the inhabitants of help from Eastern Germany. The USA are apparently organising a so-called "airlift" which just serves their purposes of propaganda.

2. How useful is **Source A** as evidence of the tensions during the Berlin Blockade? **4**

Source B was said at a public meeting by President Truman of America in 1949.

Source B

> We refused to be forced out of the city of Berlin. We demonstrated to the people of Europe that we would act and act firmly when their freedom was threatened. The airlift was a great success in supplying food and fuel to the people of Berlin. Politically, the airlift brought the people of Western Europe closer to us. The Berlin Blockade was a move by the Russians to test our ability and our will to resist.

3. Discuss the attitude of President Truman to the Berlin crisis. **4**

Source C is a Soviet commentary on the Berlin crisis.

Source C

> The crisis was planned in Washington. In 1948 there was real danger of war. The conduct of the Western powers risked bloody incidents. The self blockade of the Western powers hit the West Berlin population with harshness. The people were freezing and starving. In the spring of 1949 the USA was forced to yield—their war plans had come to nothing, because of the conduct of the USSR.

4. How far do **Sources B** and **C** agree about the Berlin crisis? **4**

[END OF CONTEXT IIC]

Marks

UNIT III—PEOPLE AND POWER

CONTEXT A: USA 1850–1880

SECTION A: KNOWLEDGE AND UNDERSTANDING

> Most Americans could not accept the Mormons as they were quite different.

1. In what ways were the Mormons different from other Americans?   3

> The Republicans fought a clear campaign that appealed to many in the North.

2. Explain the reasons why people in the North voted for the Republican Party in 1860.   4

SECTION B: ENQUIRY SKILLS

The following sources relate to the period of Reconstruction.

Study the sources carefully and answer the questions which follow.
You should use your own knowledge where appropriate.

Source A was written in a letter to President Johnson from an imprisoned Southern senator.

Source A

> You are no enemy of the South. By your wise and noble statesmanship you have become the benefactor of the Southern people in the time of their greatest need. You have entitled yourself to the gratitude of those living and those yet to live.

3. Discuss the attitude of the author of **Source A** towards President Johnson.   4

Source B describes life in the South during Reconstruction.

Source B

> New opportunities were quickly seized by the Blacks. They set up farms and businesses and went to school and university. This alarmed the Southern whites and many joined anti-Black organisations. There were murders, rapes and whippings. There was also increased discrimination as Whites gave Blacks the worst jobs. Although Blacks were entitled to vote, armed gangs of Whites sometimes stopped them.

4. How fully does **Source B** describe the problems faced by Blacks during the period of Reconstruction in the South?

    You must use **evidence from the source** and **your own knowledge** and give reasons for your answer. **5**

[END OF CONTEXT IIIA]

Marks

UNIT III—PEOPLE AND POWER

CONTEXT B: INDIA 1917–1947

SECTION A: KNOWLEDGE AND UNDERSTANDING

> Gandhi described events at Amritsar as "an act of inhumanity and vengeance".

1. Describe the events at Amritsar in April 1919.   3

> Lord Irwin, Viceroy of India announced that the Simon Commission would investigate the prospects for constitutional change in India.

2. Explain why the setting up of the Simon Commission failed to stop unrest in India.   4

SECTION B: ENQUIRY SKILLS

The following sources give evidence about Mountbatten's role in Indian independence.

Study the sources carefully and answer the questions which follow.
You should use your own knowledge where appropriate.

Source A was written by Dr Taylor who worked in Bombay when Mountbatten was Viceroy.

Source A

> We were very glad that Mountbatten came to India. He put aside all the conventions of being Viceroy and all the uniforms and parades. He was just an ordinary man and willing to meet people at their own level. This was a new idea which really touched the Indians. What pleased Nehru and Gandhi was that Mountbatten was prepared to put all ceremony aside and deal with a problem man to man.

3. Discuss the attitude of Dr Taylor to Mountbatten as Viceroy of India.   4

Marks

Source B is from a speech made by Mountbatten when India became independent on August 15th, 1947.

Source B

> I know well that the rejoicing which your freedom brings is balanced in your hearts by the sadness that it could not come to a united India. At this historic moment, let us not forget all that India owes to Mahatma Gandhi—the architect of her freedom. In your first prime Minister, Pandit Jawaharlal Nehru, you have a world renowned leader of courage and vision. His trust and friendship have helped me beyond measure.

4. How fully does **Source B** describe the background to the granting of independence to India in 1947?

   You must use **evidence from the source** and **your own knowledge** and give reasons for your answer. 5

[END OF CONTEXT IIIB]

UNIT III—PEOPLE AND POWER

CONTEXT C: RUSSIA 1914–1941

SECTION A: KNOWLEDGE AND UNDERSTANDING

> Early in 1917, Russia collapsed into Revolution.

1. Explain why revolution broke out in Russia in March 1917. **4**

> Popular discontent with War Communism convinced Lenin that a change in government economic policy was necessary.

2. Describe Lenin's New Economic Policy. **3**

SECTION B: ENQUIRY SKILLS

The following sources relate to Stalin's rule.

**Study the sources carefully and answer the questions which follow.
You should use your own knowledge where appropriate.**

Source A is an extract from Lenin's Testament which he dictated shortly before he died.

Source A

> Comrade Stalin, having become Secretary, has unlimited authority concentrated in his hands. I am not sure whether he will be capable of using that authority with sufficient caution. Stalin is too rude and this defect, although quite tolerable in our midst and in dealings between Communists, becomes intolerable in a General Secretary. For this reason, I suggest that comrades think about a way to remove Stalin from that post and replace him with someone who has greater tolerance.

3. Discuss Lenin's view of Stalin as shown in **Source A**. **4**

Marks

Source B is from "Russia and the USSR, 1905–1956" by Nigel Kelly.

Source B

> Many of those who were "purged" on Stalin's orders were loyal Communists with years of service to the party. Often they simply could not believe what was happening to them and were convinced that some terrible mistake had been made. The majority of Stalin's victims were ordinary people such as teachers and factory workers who had for some, usually unknown, reason fallen out with the authorities. Few of the victims actually wanted to overthrow Communism or replace Stalin.

4. How fully does **Source B** describe the Purges which took place under Stalin?

    You must use **evidence from the source** and **your own knowledge** and give reasons for your answer. 5

[*END OF CONTEXT IIIC*]

UNIT III—PEOPLE AND POWER

CONTEXT D: GERMANY 1918–1939

SECTION A: KNOWLEDGE AND UNDERSTANDING

> After the end of the war, there was chaos in many German cities.

1. Describe what happened during the Spartacist revolt in Berlin. **3**

> The opportunities presented by the Reichstag fire were too good for the Nazis to miss.

2. Explain why the Reichstag fire helped the Nazis. **4**

SECTION B: ENQUIRY SKILLS

The following sources are about young people in Nazi Germany.

**Study the sources carefully and answer the questions which follow.
You should use your own knowledge where appropriate.**

In **Source A**, a German writes about his memories of school days in Nazi Germany.

Source A

> Although we were meant to, no one in our class ever read Mein Kampf. I myself only took quotations down from the book. On the whole we didn't know much about Nazi ideology. Even anti-Semitism was brought in rather marginally at school. Nevertheless, we were politically programmed to obey orders, to learn the soldierly virtue of standing to attention and to stop thinking when the magic word "Fatherland" was mentioned.

3. Discuss the attitude of the author of **Source A** towards Nazi education. **4**

Source B is a photograph of members of the Hitler Youth in the 1930s.

Source B

4. How fully does **Source B** show why children were attracted to Nazi Youth organisations?

   You must use **evidence from the source** and **your own knowledge** and give reasons for your answer.

   5

[END OF CONTEXT IIID]

[END OF QUESTION PAPER]

[BLANK PAGE]

[BLANK PAGE]

Pocket answer section for SQA Standard Grade History General and Credit Levels 2001 to 2003

© 2003 Scottish Qualifications Authority, All Rights Reserved
Published by Leckie & Leckie Ltd, 8 Whitehill Terrace, St Andrews, Scotland, KY16 8RN
tel: 01334 475656, fax: 01334 477392, enquiries@leckieandleckie.co.uk, www.leckieandleckie.co.uk

Marking at General Level

Marks should be awarded to the candidate for:
carrying out the correct process
using relevant presented evidence
using relevant recall.

Section A (Knowledge and Understanding)

All answers to items in Section A of the paper **must** make use of at least one piece of relevant recall to obtain full marks.

A *selection* of possible recall is given in the Marking Instructions. The marker will use professional judgement to determine the relevance of other possible recall.

The use of duly selected, presented evidence is permitted. Only where a candidate has **done nothing at all** with presented evidence should it then be regarded as simply copying.

Section B (Enquiry Skills)

In Section B (Enquiry Skills) any item which requires the use of relevant recall is clearly indicated and full marks can only be awarded to those items when such recall is used.

At General Level, in an ES1 item it is not enough to state that a source is useful as it is a "primary source" or that it was "written at the time (of the investigation)". In order to attract a mark the candidate must relate this statement directly to the source.

Examples:

This source is useful as it is written at the time (of the investigation). = 0 marks

This source is reliable as it was written by a man living then (at the time). = 0 marks

This source is valuable as it was written during the period under investigation. = 0 marks

In a K3 question a candidate should be credited for either explaining the importance of the factors in the presented evidence and/or by assessing the relative importance of relevant, recalled evidence.

It is now acceptable (and worthy of a mark) if a candidate evaluates a source and correctly identifies its use as:

"written at the time of the investigation/issue/topic under discussion"

"written during the time period under investigation"

"written by someone who was actually there at the time."

At General Level the correct demonstration of process or application of judgement where required **must be automatically rewarded** *if reinforced* with relevant and appropriate evidence:

Examples:

This source is useful as it was written during a period of great changes in farming in the late 18th century. = 2 marks

This source is useful as it comes from an official government report. = 2 marks

I agree that machinery improved coal mining as it increased productivity. = 2 marks

Sources C and D agree that the Germans felt angry at the Treaty of Versailles. = 2 marks

In all ES1 (source evaluation responses) the **ideal**, developed response concerning the contemporaneity of the source is given. It is sufficient however, for 1 mark, **at General Level**, for a student to respond that a source is useful as "it is a primary source, written at the time".

In an ES2 question 1 mark is given for a simple comparison and 2 marks for a developed point. Examples are given in the Marking Instructions.

In an ES4 item asking the candidate to put a source into its historical context, full marks cannot be awarded unless relevant recall is given.

In order to obtain **full** marks, an item which requires the suggestion of a conclusion (ES6 item: ie Q.5 in Unit 1) must use presented evidence **and** recalled evidence. Any response based on either presented evidence **only** or recalled evidence **only** may attract a maximum of 2 marks, even if the process is correct.

(A response giving three points of recall and one piece of presented evidence = 4 marks

A response giving three points of presented evidence and one piece of recall = 4 marks)

The abbreviations K1 – K3, and E1 – E6 used above indicate the particular sub skills of the extended EGRC to which an individual question relates:

K1: description; K2: explanation; K3: importance;
ES1: evaluation; ES2: comparison; ES3: point of view; ES4: set in context; ES5: select evidence; ES6: present conclusion.

In an ES5 item (selection of evidence) listing or copying of relevant evidence from the presented source(s) is allowed and should be fully credited. Recall or personal judgement cannot be credited in this item.

History General Level

INTRODUCTION

Knowledge and Understanding
Answers are given as bullet points. Candidates must always respond in full sentences, addressing the correct process and actually responding to the item: either describing, explaining or assessing importance (preferably with reference to other important factors).

In the 8 mark, extended writing exercise the candidate should structure the response appropriately with an introduction, six points of relevant, supporting evidence and a conclusion which clearly addresses the specific requirements of the item.

Enquiry Skills
Evaluation of evidence: normally, only 1 mark will be allocated for each type of evaluation offered: contemporaneity; authorship; content; purpose etc.
Comparing Sources: 1 mark is allocated for a simple comparison; 2 marks for a developed comparison. Examples of both types are given.
Assessing attitude: 1 mark is allocated for each assessment or explanation.
Putting a source in context: full marks can only be awarded if recall is used.
Selecting evidence to address an issue: this is the only area where a candidate can supply bullet points or list evidence.
Providing a conclusion: full marks cannot be awarded unless the candidate uses presented evidence + recall + balance in their response.

History General Level—2001

Unit I—Context A: 1750s–1850s
Section A

1. The candidate explains the effects of better farming technology using evidence such as:
   - new technology replaced wind power
   - Meikle's threshing machine replaced the unpredictable use of the wind
   - Small's plough cut the soil easily
   - Small's machine had a metal cutting blade
   - Small's plough could be pulled by just 2 horses

   and from recall such as:
   - old hand-labour, winnowing techniques
   - old threshing methods using the flail
   - Meikle's machine used mechanical flails
   - new technology saved time
   - new technology saved human effort
   - old ploughs: wooden, clumsy, pulled by team of oxen
   - seed drills replacing broadcast sowing
   - scythe replacing sickle
   - reaping machines slowly replacing scythe
   - farmers could choose when to perform farming tasks

2. The candidate assesses the importance of good water supplies using evidence such as:
   - pumps were much used (by many people)
   - water was often polluted
   - cholera was caused by polluted water
   - 50,000 died of cholera in 1848

   and **recalled evidence** such as:
   - bad water spread disease/killed people
   - existing water supply was insufficient
   - bad sanitation affected water supplies
   - infected sewage found its way into the water supply
   - overcrowding and poor living conditions also spread disease
   - houses had no running water
   - lack of medical knowledge meant disease from bad water was usually fatal

Section B

3. The candidate evaluates Source C using **evidence** such as:
   - authorship:
     eyewitness account of changes in food supply
   - contemporaneity:
     primary source from someone living in the early 19th Century
   - content:
     useful content on changes in food supply and infant mortality
   - purpose:
     designed to inform as a memory of life at a time of change
   - accuracy:
     written as an autobiography, looking back, so could be affected by memory
   - limitation:
     only one man's account of one area **or** only one cause of population growth

4. The candidate selects evidence for the issue from Source C, such as:
   - food supplies in the 1760s were poor
   - little meat and few vegetables in 1760s
   - people ate very little before improvements in food took place by 1814
   - people ate better by 1814
   - more babies were born healthy in 1814
   - fewer babies died in 1814

   The candidate selects evidence to show other factors from Source D, such as:
   - demand for labour (more children are needed)
   - rise in the birth rate
   - earlier marriages and thus more children
   - better wages meant people could afford children
   - advances in hygiene
   - advances in medical care

5. The candidate agrees or disagrees that the population of Scotland rose between 1760 and 1820 as a result of improvements in food supply using the evidence presented above and from relevant, recalled evidence such as:

   For the issue:
   - fall in the death rate
   - results of new farming
   - nutrition from potatoes, vegetables
   - exponential increase—population explosion

5. (continued)

for other factors:
- increase in desire to have children (better conditions; country at peace)
- control of disease (smallpox)
- disappearance of disease (plague; malaria)
- better child care
- better hospital facilities
- control of drinking
- lack of contraception

Unit I—Context B: 1830s–1930s
Section A

1. The candidate explains the ways in which rail travel improved between 1850 and 1930 using **presented evidence** such as:
   - average speeds increased (to 60 mph)
   - London to Aberdeen took only 8·5 hours (62 mph)
   - locomotives improved
   - railway competition encouraged improvements
   - heating introduced into carriages

   and **recalled evidence** such as:
   - earlier speeds were slower
   - earlier conditions were primitive
   - lavatories introduced into some trains
   - sleeping cars introduced
   - restaurant cars introduced
   - improvements made to carriage design
   - lighting introduced into carriages
   - better track and signalling
   - Tay Bridge and Forth Bridge reduced travelling time North
   - locomotive technology improved

2. The candidate assesses the importance of the lack of clean water using **presented evidence** such as:
   - people unable to wash without clean water
   - typhus results from dirty conditions/lice
   - typhus killed many people
   - cholera and typhoid fever caused by contaminated water
   - over 100,000 people killed by cholera
   - polluted food also killed people

   and **recalled evidence** such as:
   - houses did not have running water
   - water often had to be bought
   - open sewers polluted water supply
   - lack of sewers and drains
   - further connection between cholera and polluted water
   - early Public Health Acts ineffective
   - other possible causes of disease/ill health

Section B

3. The candidate evaluates Source C using **evidence** such as:
   - authorship:
     Scottish eyewitness account
   - contemporaneity:
     primary source from period of population growth in 19th Century
   - content:
     useful information on diet and population

3. (continued)

   - purpose:
     A Reminiscence: to inform others
   - accuracy:
     memoir of one individual who experienced the events
     a memory of events: possible flaw
   - limitation:
     just one area of Scotland covered/one person's opinion

4. The candidate identifies evidence for the issue from Source C, such as:
   - eating habits have changed
   - diet improved: more meat, vegetables
   - more food available: more baker's shops
   - people are healthier
   - people are living longer
   - families are larger

   The candidate identifies other factors from Source D, such as:
   - declining death rate
   - drop in infant mortality
   - mothers healthier
   - general improvement in standard of health
   - babies healthier
   - more babies surviving

5. The candidate suggests a conclusion using the evidence presented above and from relevant, recalled evidence such as:

   For the issue:
   - better farming methods
   - developments in railways for transporting food
   - greater choice of food

   } Resulting in healthier population, people living longer, larger families

   for other factors:
   - better medicine: vaccination
   - better child care
   - disappearance of some diseases
   - better living conditions: sewerage; water supply
   - Public Health Acts
   - better hygiene: cotton clothes; soap

Unit I—Context C: 1880s–Present Day
Section A

1. The candidate explains how motor transport has affected lives in the countryside using **presented evidence** such as:
   - rural folk/people from the countryside can visit towns
   - children can go to school by bus
   - Doctors can visit countryside (to treat people)
   - roads have been built in the countryside
   - beauty spots have been damaged
   - motor accidents
   - problem with safety on the roads
   - cars make people lazy

   and **recalled evidence** such as:
   - fresh food can be delivered
   - people can commute
   - farmers can take produce to market
   - pollution problems
   - traffic jams

History General Level—2001 (cont.)

2. The candidate assesses the importance of clean water using **presented evidence** such as:
   - would help to stop disease spreading
   - water has to be clean and free from disease
   - sewage must not contaminate water
   - sewerage also important
   - by 1900 most towns had a clean supply

   and **recalled evidence** such as:
   - cholera and typhoid further reduced
   - other factors are important: housing; medical care; hygiene.

Section B

3. The candidate evaluates Source C using **evidence** such as:
   - authorship:
     well informed reporter
   - contemporaneity:
     primary source from 1960—during period of population rise in question
   - purpose:
     designed to inform—to record facts
   - content:
     links diet to population growth
   - accuracy:
     unlikely to be biased—a statistical account: accurate figures
   - limitation:
     figures for Aberdeenshire towns only; only 1 factor mentioned.

4. The candidate selects evidence for the issue from Source C, such as:
   - town dwellers better fed
   - more money was spent on food
   - more fruit in the diet
   - school meals
   - free milk
   - uncontaminated milk available

   The candidate selects other evidence from Source D, such as:
   - babies live beyond 1 year (infant mortality dropped)
   - TB reduced
   - antibiotics available
   - fewer mothers died at childbirth
   - women went on to have families

5. The candidate suggests a conclusion supported by presented evidence such as that above and from relevant, recalled evidence such as:
   - food transport
   - farming improvements
   - other health factors: eg inoculation
   - better hospital treatment
   - National Health improvements
   - movement into towns
   - immigration
   - improved hygiene: use of soap, disinfectant

Unit II—Context A: 1790s–1820s

Section A

1. The candidate assesses the importance of Nelson's contribution to victory at sea using **presented evidence** such as:
   - destroyed the French fleet at Aboukir
   - gained control of the Mediterranean sea for Britain
   - captured island of Minorca (strategic naval base)

   and from **recalled evidence** such as:
   - defeated Danish navy at Copenhagen
   - brought about collapse of the Armed Neutrality against Britain
   - destroyed French fleet at Trafalgar
   - confirmed supremacy of British sea power
   - Nelson personally supplied leadership and charisma
   - other factors which contributed to Britain's victory at sea

2. The candidate describes conditions for British sailors using **presented evidence** such as:
   - poor diet
   - frequent outbreaks of illness/disease/scurvy
   - little fresh air below decks
   - damp, overcrowded conditions
   - poor hygiene
   - poor washing facilities

   and from **recalled evidence** such as:
   - lack of vitamins in the diet
   - water often undrinkable
   - no toilet facilities
   - poor/erratic pay
   - dangerous conditions, especially during fighting
   - harsh discipline

Section B

3. The candidate states the attitudes of the French as shown in Source C using **evidence** such as:
   - **worry** that the war was going badly
   - **concern** at the difficulties war caused
   - **concern** at high prices of food
   - **angry** at bank notes losing value

4. The candidate evaluates the completeness of the sources with reference to **presented evidence** such as:
   - famine
   - growth of crime
   - high unemployment
   - collapse of industry

   and from **recalled evidence** such as:
   - high food prices
   - shortages of food
   - inflation/money lost its value
   - production of assignats
   - conscription of troops
   - Reign of Terror instituted
   - wages kept low by law
   - death penalty heavily enforced
   - rebellion against government (eg in Gironde and Western France)
   - foreign armies invading France

Unit II—Context B: 1890s–1920s

Section A

1. The candidate describes fighting in the First World War using **presented evidence** such as:
   - use of trenches
   - shrapnel shells
   - use of troops going into a frontal attack
   - heavy casualties resulted

   and from **recalled evidence** such as:
   - artillery barrage
   - troops going "over the top"
   - details of trench warfare
   - machine guns
   - other weapons: eg rifles, grenades
   - assault on enemy positions
   - new technology: gas, tanks
   - ineffectiveness of frontal attacks
   - use of barbed wire

2. The candidate assesses the importance of Clemenceau's views on how Germany should be treated, using **presented evidence** such as:
   - his anti-German attitude was important
   - he decided that Germany should be told what to do
   - he wanted to treat Germany firmly
   - he wanted to make sure France would not be invaded again

   and from **recalled evidence** such as:
   - he was one of the Big Four who negotiated the treatment of Germany
   - Germany was severely treated
   - Germany was dictated to (by the Diktat)
   - examples of severe treatment of Germany
   - examples of attempts to keep Germany weak
   - contribution of other important representatives at Versailles
   - Wilson's more idealistic approach overshadowed by Clemenceau's views

Section B

3. The candidate determines the attitudes which the poster (Source C) is encouraging with reference to **presented evidence** such as:
   - Britain is the cause of continued fighting
   - Britain is causing suffering
   - Britain is stopping them living their lives in peace
   - Britain is their deadly enemy
   - Together, Germans can still win the war/beat Britain

4. The candidate assesses the completeness of Source D with reference to **presented evidence** such as:
   - a lot of turnips eaten
   - luxury goods disappeared
   - rich could still afford luxuries
   - necessities rationed/soap rationed

   and from **recalled evidence** such as:
   - effects of the blockade
   - further effects of rationing
   - food riots
   - use of ersatz food
   - horrors of air-raids
   - loss of relatives
   - problems caused by inflation
   - effects of (Spanish) influenza

Unit II—Context C: 1930s–1960s

Section A

1. The candidate assesses the importance of Churchill's leadership using **presented evidence** such as:
   - he was in charge of defence
   - he inspected fortifications
   - he started the Home Guard
   - he gave lots of orders

   and **recalled evidence** such as:
   - his speeches boosted morale
   - he negotiated US aid (lend-lease)
   - the coalition government united the country
   - and other possible factors, eg:
   - RAF defeated Luftwaffe in Battle of Britain
   - air-raid precautions and evacuations helped protect civilians

2. The candidate describes the effects of the atomic bomb using **presented evidence** such as:
   - light burned eyes
   - people incinerated
   - 70,000 killed

   and **recalled evidence** such as:
   - many survivors burned
   - blast destroyed most of city
   - thousands died from radiation sickness
   - contributed to surrender of Japan
   - started nuclear age/arms race

Section B

3. The candidate evaluates the attitude of Germans as shown in Source C using such evidence as:
   - thought the situation was dreadful
   - alarmed at no public services working (gas, electricity, water)
   - panic amidst the chaos
   - only thought was to escape
   - thought the situation was frightening/terrifying

4. The candidate evaluates the completeness of the source with reference to **presented evidence** such as:
   - some did feel the war was ending
   - some felt that Hitler would lose
   - some felt that Nazism should be abandoned
   - some felt Nazis were criminals
   - some felt Nazis should be opposed/resisted

   and from **recalled evidence** such as:
   - typical of some feeling in 1943
   - some earlier attitudes were optimistic
   - typical of those who resisted the Nazis: religious groups; youth groups; July Bomb plotters
   - air raids did affect morale
   - many Germans still continued to support the war effort
   - most Germans did not support resistance
   - many were frightened to oppose the Nazis
   - Nazi regime made opposition difficult

History General Level—2001 (cont.)

Unit III—Context A: USA 1850–1880
Section A

1. The candidate describes the attitude of native Americans (Indians) to the land using **presented evidence** such as:
   - land is very valuable
   - land cannot be destroyed (is there forever)
   - land gives life (in the same way as the sun and water)
   - land cannot be sold

   and from **recalled evidence** such as:
   - given by the Great White Spirit
   - everyone should only take what they need from the land
   - everyone should live in harmony with the land
   - land should not be exploited
   - land belongs to no one
   - land was held in trust

2. The candidate explains why slavery was a cause of the Civil War using **presented evidence** such as:
   - southern, slave owning states fighting for right to manage own affairs
   - northern states were opposed to slavery
   - southern states wanted to opt out of the Union
   - northern states determined to preserve the Union

   and from **recalled evidence** such as:
   - north was generally abolitionist
   - horrors of slave life
   - economic differences between industrial North and plantation South
   - fears about destruction of Southern way of life
   - fanatical leaders unwilling to compromise

Section B

3. The candidate evaluates Source C using evidence such as:
   - authorship:
     newspaper cartoon: sympathetic to Blacks/against White terrorism
   - contemporaneity:
     primary source from 1873—at time of Reconstruction/White terrorism
   - content:
     shows Blacks are being oppressed/methods of white terrorists
   - accuracy:
     northern newspaper: hostile to KKK and White terrorists
   - purpose:
     to criticise treatment of Blacks in the Reconstruction South
   - reliability:
     content matches other evidence: KKK carrying weapons, lynchings . . .

4. The candidate assesses the completeness of Source C using **presented evidence** such as:
   - show typical costume of the KKK: white hoods etc
   - shows KKK smiling: happy in his work?
   - shows KKK heavily armed
   - shows KKK dealing in death (hand on skull)
   - shows KKK in league with other white supremacists (White League)
   - shows KKK suppressing the Blacks

   and from **recalled evidence** such as:
   - KKK usually shown as grim terrorists
   - does not show other KKK symbols: fiery cross
   - does not show clandestine/secret nature of the organisation
   - KKK usually operated at night
   - no evidence of hierarchy/rank/senior members
   - no evidence of social background of KKK

5. The candidate assesses agreement between the Sources with reference to features such as:

   Both sources agree that KKK used terror against Blacks:
   - Source D says "set up to terrorise Black people"
   - Source C shows Blacks cowering beneath armed KKK figure

   Both sources agree that arson was used against Black people:
   - Source D says KKK "did not hesitate at arson"
   - Source C shows burning building

   Both sources agree that schools for Black people were attacked:
   - Source D says "favourite target was burning local school"
   - Source C shows school house in flames (and a discarded school book)

   Both sources say hanging was used against the Blacks:
   - Source D says "Many Blacks were hanged"
   - Source C shows a hanging body

   Both sources agree about how KKK dressed:
   - Source D says "ghostly white clothes"
   - Source C shows figure in white, hooded sheet

   Both sources agree about the secrecy of the KKK:
   - Source D says "secret society"
   - Source C shows hooded (clandestine) figure

   Only Source D says KKK frightened Blacks by carrying a burning cross

   Only Source D says torture was used

   Only Source C says Blacks were being treated worse than when they were slaves

Unit III—Context B: India 1917–1947
Section A

1. The candidate explains why British control of India was of benefit, using **presented evidence** such as:
   - an important part of the British Empire
   - supplied many Indian goods which were exported to Britain
   - enabled many British goods to be sent to India
   - Britain's largest single market
   - British cotton and/or heavy engineering products were sent to India

   and **recalled evidence** such as:
   - examples of Indian goods sent to Britain (cotton, rice, jute, tea, wheat)
   - provided employment
   - provided jobs in the Raj

1. (continued)
- non-economic reasons: racial superiority/ imperialism "civilising mission"

2. The candidate describes the events at Amritsar using **presented evidence** such as:
   - took place in the Jallianwalla Bagh
   - 10,000 demonstrators met British troops
   - a massacre happened

   and **recalled evidence** such as:
   - British troops commanded by General Dyer
   - Dyer acting on orders of British Governor
   - British army opened fire without warning
   - Indian crowd was unarmed
   - crowd was protesting for home rule
   - incident took place in the knowledge of previous violence (4 Europeans killed)
   - many Indians were unaware of extended laws/martial law
   - result was 379 Indians killed; 1208 wounded

Section B
3. The candidate evaluates Source C using evidence such as:
   - authorship:
     an actual Muslim League poster
   - contemporaneity:
     published in 1946: the year of Direct Action Day
   - content:
     shows areas claimed by the Muslim League
   - purpose:
     reveals feelings and intentions of Muslim League (emotive language)
   - limitation:
     map does not show that some of claimed areas were mixed Hindu/Muslim (eg Punjab, Bengal)
   - accuracy:
     shows attitude of most Muslims

4. The candidate assesses the completeness of Source C with reference to such **presented evidence** as:
   - reveals attitudes of Muslims
   - shows Muslims wanted partition
   - shows Muslims were prepared to fight and die for Partition
   - shows the areas in which Muslims wanted to break away from India

   and from **recalled evidence** such as:
   - does not reveal Hindu attitudes
   - does not reveal complications caused by divisions in caste, wealth, religion, language
   - does not reveal attitude of British in India
   - does not reveal attitude of Sikhs
   - does not show problems over alignment of proposed borders
   - does not reveal attitude of people in the Punjab or Bengal

5. The candidate compares agreement/disagreement between the sources with reference to features such as:

   The sources agree that Muslims were encouraged to fight for Pakistan:
   - Source C: "We shall fight for Pakistan"
   - Source D: "Leaders encouraged Muslims to fight"

5. (continued)
The sources agree (to some extent) about deaths:
- Source C: "We shall die; take it or perish"
- Source D mentions 5000 deaths in Calcutta
- only Source D describes Muslim attacks on Hindus
- only Source D describes Muslims looting Indian shops
- only Source D mentions it provoked Hindu retaliation

Unit III—Context C: Russia 1914–1941
Section A
1. The candidate explains why the Tsar had so much power using **presented evidence** such as:
   - he was chief of the armed forces
   - he was head of the Orthodox Church
   - he was believed to be chosen by God

   and **recalled evidence** such as:
   - he was an autocrat—could rule as he wished
   - he had no parliament to control his power
   - he used the Okhrana, secret police, which crushed opposition
   - censorship of newspapers and books
   - used army/Cossacks to crush unrest
   - exiled opponents to Siberia
   - most Russians belonged to Orthodox Church (and accepted Tsar's powerful position)

2. The candidate describes the way civilians suffered during the Civil War using **presented evidence** such as:
   - thousands of workers shot
   - peasants flogged
   - widespread looting

   and **recalled evidence** such as:
   - women publicly flogged
   - peasants' crops burned
   - widespread famine
   - food rationing introduced in towns
   - many villages and homes destroyed
   - many forced to go and fight

Section B
3. The candidate evaluates the source using evidence such as:
   - authorship:
     from official government figures/a graph easy to "read"
   - contemporaneity:
     figures from within the period of NEP
   - content:
     shows that production did increase 1922–25
   - accuracy:
     possible government propaganda
   - purpose:
     figures aimed to show that NEP was working
   - limitation:
     only shows some areas of productivity

History General Level—2001 (cont.)

4. The candidate assesses the completeness of the evidence in Source C using **presented evidence** such as:
   - iron production increased
   - grain production increased
   - cattle increased in number
   - NEP partly successful
   - more cattle in 1925 than pre-war
   - iron production did not increase to pre-war figure
   - grain production did not increase to pre-war figure

   and from **recalled evidence** such as:
   - land under cultivation increased
   - Kulaks did particularly well
   - starvation became less of a problem
   - foreign specialists recruited
   - other industrial production did not increase to pre-war figures
   - Russia did not fully catch up with the West
   - concentration on heavy industry (but it did not recover)
   - NEP men encouraged private trade
   - light industry improved due to increased consumer demand

5. The candidate compares the effects of the NEP as shown in Sources C and D using evidence such as:

   Sources agree that animal production increased after 1922:
   - Source C shows an increase from 45 m to 62 m
   - Source D says more animals appeared

   Sources agree that industrial output increased after 1922:
   - Source C shows iron production increasing
   - Source D says industrial production began to climb

   Sources agree that food production improved:
   - Source C shows increase in grain/cattle
   - Source D says that starvation was less of a problem

   Sources disagree that grain production increased to pre World War One levels:
   - Source C shows that by 1925, grain had not reached level of 1913
   - Source D says that grain production was back to 1913 level

   Only Source D mentions enthusiasm of the peasants/workers

Unit III—Context D: Germany 1918–1939
Section A

1. The candidate describes the aftermath of the Munich Putsch using **presented evidence** such as:
   - Hitler accused of high treason
   - Hitler put on trial
   - Hitler's trial lasted 24 days
   - Hitler made front page news
   - Hitler's words were read by millions

   and **recalled evidence** such as:
   - Hitler was arrested
   - Hitler sentenced to five years
   - Hitler imprisoned in Landsberg Castle

1. (continued)
   - Hitler spent 9 months in prison
   - Hitler wrote Mein Kampf while in prison
   - Hitler decided to use more political methods

2. The candidate explains why the Weimar Republic was unpopular in 1932 using **presented evidence** such as:
   - could not solve unemployment
   - new elections did not help/democracy was weak
   - blamed for Versailles
   - criticised by Hitler

   and **recalled evidence** such as:
   - many blamed Weimar for defeat in World War One
   - many blamed Weimar for accepting reparations
   - many blamed Weimar for inflation
   - many people preferred Nazi policies

Section B

3. The candidate assesses the usefulness of Source C in terms of evidence such as:
   - authorship:
     produced by Nazis
   - contemporaneity:
     primary source produced during the Nazi era
   - content:
     useful detail relating to the activities of Hitler Youth members
   - purpose:
     to persuade young people to join the movement
   - accuracy:
     Nazi propaganda—everyone enjoying themselves
   - consistency/limitation:
     backed up/contradicted by other evidence: eg compulsion to join

4. The candidate compares agreement in the sources using evidence such as:

   Both sources agree that there was a range/variety of activities:
   - Source C shows a lot of activities
   - Source D says "range of activities"

   Both sources agree that members wore (were pleased to wear) uniforms:
   - Source C shows children (proudly?) in uniform
   - Source D says "some enjoyed the uniforms"

   Both sources agree that marching and discipline took place:
   - Source C shows a group marching in order
   - Source D says "children enjoyed marching and discipline"

   Both sources agree that Hitler Youth went camping:
   - Source C shows tents/campers
   - Source D says "outdoor events such as camping"

   Both sources agree about appeal of musical events/parades:
   - Source C shows drums/marching
   - Source D says "music was . . . part of parades"

5. The candidate assesses the completeness of Source D using **presented evidence** such as:
   - Hitler Youth offered outdoor activities
   - Hitler Youth activities were exciting
   - Nazi youth movements involved attractive pursuits
   - Hitler Youth members wore uniforms
   - some enjoyed drill and some marching/military activities
   - some enjoyed (military) music

   and from **recalled evidence** such as:
   - Hitler Pimpfen attracted young members
   - League of German Maidens attracted girls
   - girls trained to be good Aryan mothers
   - Nazi Education/teachers
   - Nazi propaganda
   - brainwashing into Nazi ideology

History General Level—2002

Unit I—Context A: 1750s–1850s

Section A

1. The candidate explains why the population increased using **presented evidence** such as:
   - fall in the death rate
   - no famines
   - no serious epidemics of disease
   - better standard of living

   and **recalled evidence** such as:
   - earlier marriages: larger families
   - shorter apprenticeships leading to early marriage
   - better housing conditions/sanitation = less disease
   - better hygiene
   - advances in medical knowledge
   - farming improvements and better diet
   - decrease in infant mortality

2. The candidate describes changes brought about by the 1832 Reform Act in Scotland using **presented evidence** such as:
   - corrected worst faults of old system
   - burgh vote given to shopkeepers and skilled workers
   - wealthy farmers in counties got the vote
   - middle class gained political power

   and **recalled evidence** such as:
   - many more men gained vote
   - town councils lost power monopoly
   - burgh franchise = £10·00 property owner
   - county vote given to £10·00 land-owner
   - county vote to £50·00 renter
   - seats more fairly distributed
   - more seats to industrialised towns
   - 8 more MPs given to Scotland
   - uniform voting qualification in English boroughs
   - rotten boroughs abolished

Section B

3. The candidate evaluates **Source C** using evidence such as:
   - contemporaneity: written during the period of major change in Scottish (farming)

3. (continued)
   - authorship: written by an improver; a titled landowner; an MP: in (a report)
   - content: praises the advantages of agricultural machinery
   - accuracy: possible bias from an enthusiastic improver/agrees with other evidence that machines helped farming
   - purpose: written to persuade others to improve
   - limitation: only one man's opinion

4. The candidate identifies evidence of agreement in **Source C** such as:
   - threshing mills were an advantage
   - amount of manual labour was reduced
   - more food being produced for Scotland
   - easier to run Scottish farms

   The candidate identifies evidence of disagreement in **Source D** such as:
   - poorer tenants lost their land
   - machines led to Scots workers losing jobs
   - disappearance of small tenant farmer
   - many Scots reduced to begging
   - some Scots forced to leave the countryside to find work
   - some Scottish villages became deserted

5. The candidate comes to a conclusion on whether changes in agriculture were good for Scotland using evidence such as:

   from **presented evidence**:
   - work could be done more easily
   - more food was produced

   BUT
   - tenants lost their land
   - farm workers lost their jobs
   - labourers faced poverty
   - villages were emptied

   and from **recalled evidence** such as:
   - farm work was made easier
   - machines such as new ploughs, reapers etc cut down on work
   - Scottish lairds got wealthier
   - many tenant farmers became rich
   - Scotland's growing population was fed
   - standards of living/housing for Scots got better

   BUT
   - some workers were evicted (in the Highlands—Clearances)
   - landlords were able to ask for higher rents

Unit I—Context B: 1830s–1930s

Section A

1. The candidate explains the reasons why the population grew using **presented evidence** such as:
   - better diet
   - less overcrowding
   - greater cleanliness
   - medical treatment

   and **recalled evidence** such as:
   - increased birth rate
   - earlier marriages: having babies younger
   - decreasing infant mortality

History General Level—2002 (cont.)

1. (continued)
- better housing
- improved sanitation
- clean water
- Irish immigration

2. The candidate describes changes to voting between 1850 and 1930 using **presented evidence** such as:
   - by 1868 230,000 men could vote
   - by 1868 skilled workmen could vote
   - by 1884 farm workers could vote
   - by 1884 some (unskilled) working class men (crofters and miners) could vote

   and **recalled evidence** such as:
   - Ballot Act, 1872 (voting was secret)
   - by 1918—all men over 21 could vote, eg: men previously excluded: male servants; soldiers in barracks; sons at home
   - by 1918—women over 30, householders, married to householders or graduates could vote
   - by 1928—all women over 21 could vote

Section B

3. The candidate evaluates **Source C** using evidence such as:
   - contemporaneity: primary source from period of railway development
   - authorship: writer in a Railway Magazine; informed journalist; a railway enthusiast
   - content: details of benefits railways have brought
   - accuracy: eye witness account/biased in favour of railways
   - purpose: to praise railways/to itemise many uses
   - limitation: omits objections to railways; one person's view

4. The candidate identifies evidence from **Source C** to show railways were good for Scotland such as:
   - express trains: fast travel to Edinburgh/Glasgow
   - travellers/holidaymakers (15,000 from Glasgow in one week)
   - movement of animals/livestock
   - transporting of fresh fish
   - Aberdeen station was busy

   The candidate identifies evidence from **Source D** to show that railways were not good for Scotland such as:
   - some disliked Sunday travel
   - concerns over pollution
   - threatened the coaching trade

5. The candidate offers a conclusion to the issue using evidence such as:

   from **presented evidence**:
   - ease/speed of transport for travellers/holidaymakers
   - (fresh) fish deliveries
   - movement of commodities/livestock

   BUT
   - some people objected to Sunday travel
   - there were pollution concerns
   - the coaching trade was threatened

5. (continued)
and from **recalled evidence** such as:
- fresh food was transported
- milk deliveries
- deliveries of mail/newspapers
- towns developed around railways
- factories were built nearby railways
- tourists/holidaymakers could use railways
- holidays by the seaside increased
- suburban living increased
- employment opportunities provided
- standard time set
- travel became increasingly comfortable

BUT
- some objected to the effect on livestock
- other occupations were affected (stables; coaching inns; canals)
- some areas were affected by railway construction
- health fears
- sparks (from locomotives) set fire to crops/banking

Unit I—Context C: 1880s–Present Day
Section A

1. The candidate explains why Scotland's population continued to grow after 1880 using **presented evidence** such as:
   - medical improvements reduced death rate
   - better housing helped to stop spread of disease
   - healthier diet caused population to rise/reduced deaths
   - people were living longer (more old folk)

   and **recalled evidence** such as:
   - earlier marriages
   - larger families
   - fall in infant mortality
   - more cures for childhood diseases: TB; polio; measles; etc
   - development of medical treatments: X rays; vaccinations; antibiotics etc
   - beginning of Welfare State: medical inspection; school meals
   - NHS care
   - free milk; health visitors etc
   - council houses of the 1930s were cleaner
   - improved domestic facilities: water supply/sanitation
   - improved hygiene/health awareness
   - improvements in transport led to better/fresher food supply
   - immigration from Ireland, Poland, Italy, Asia etc

2. The candidate describes changes in voting between 1900 and 1969 using **presented evidence** such as:
   - vote given to women (1918)
   - vote given to women over 21 (1928)
   - before 1918 no women could vote

   and **recalled evidence** such as:
   - vote given to women over 30 (1918)
   - wives of householders (1918)
   - all men over 21 (1918)
   - previously excluded group given the vote such as:
     - soldiers in barracks;
     - sons at home;
     - paupers
   - plural voting ended (1948)
   - all men and women over 18 given the vote (1969)

Section B

3. The candidate evaluates **Source C** using evidence such as:

   - contemporaneity: from the period of road building/motorway madness in 1960s
   - authorship: first hand evidence from someone with direct experience/eyewitness
   - content: gives evidence of redevelopment due to motorway building
   - accuracy: possibility of bias: one-sided account; possibility of exaggeration; based on memory
   - purpose: to protest about redevelopment/loss of old residence
   - limitation: only refers to Glasgow; only negative effects

4. The candidate identifies evidence of disagreement in **Source C** such as:
   - criticism of redevelopment for motorways
   - critical of demolition of streets/tenements
   - critical of good buildings being demolished to make way for a motorway
   - criticises council for their actions in constructing M8
   - people forced out of their houses
   - motorways are noisy

   The candidate identifies evidence of agreement in **Source D** such as:
   - increased personal freedom (petrol vehicles have brought freedom)
   - increased leisure opportunities (petrol vehicles have brought fun)
   - increased recreational travel (city people can get quickly into the country)
   - reduced price of goods
   - creation of employment
   - improved communication for rural communities

5. The candidate offers a conclusion to the issue using **presented evidence** such as:
   - freedom to travel
   - increased leisure pursuits
   - cheaper goods in shops
   - more jobs
   - improved communications
   - brings remote areas in touch

   BUT
   - motorways are noisy
   - improvements came at a price for evicted tenants
   - old communities/good buildings were destroyed

   and from **recalled evidence** such as:
   - examples of transport employment: constructing cars; driving lorries; buses
   - benefits to other industries: rubber; glass; electrics
   - bus services provided
   - door to door deliveries
   - benefits to farmers
   - industrial use
   - increase growth of suburbs: workers no longer need to live near workplace

5. (continued)
   - growth in motoring holidays
   - ability to travel into towns

   BUT
   - road deaths increased
   - landscape altered by roads and petrol stations; roundabouts etc
   - huge cost of road building and maintenance
   - traffic jams/one way streets
   - increased air pollution
   - parking problems
   - decline of city centres; out of town commuting and shopping
   - end of trams
   - rail services affected

Unit II—Context A: 1790s–1820s
Section A

1. The candidate explains the reasons for Britain and France going to war using **presented evidence** such as:
   - execution of Louis XVI seen as barbaric
   - king's death seen as unjustified
   - execution seen as a threat to all monarchs
   - Britain protested and France declared war on Britain

   and **recalled evidence** such as:
   - concern at speed of revolution beyond French borders
   - French control of Antwerp and mouth of River Scheldt: alarms British
   - Edict of Fraternity

2. The candidate explains the importance of food supply problems using **presented evidence** such as:
   - great rise in cost of living
   - difficult to import wheat
   - rise in bread prices
   - wheat prices tripled in 22 years

   and **recalled evidence** such as:
   - increased taxation to pay for war
   - effects of Continental Systems
   - effects of introduction of machinery in agriculture and industry
   - other problems existed: eg Press gangs

Section B

3. The candidate evaluates the usefulness of **Source C** using evidence such as:

   - contemporaneity: cartoon from time of Fourth Coalition
   - authorship: 19th century British artist
   - content: shows Napoleon surrounded by enemies (Fourth Coalition)
   - accuracy/bias: anti-French bias
   - purpose: to ridicule Napoleon
   - limitation: more evidence required for details of Fourth Coalition

4. The candidate evaluates the degree of agreement between **Sources C** and **D** using evidence such as:

   sources agree that Napoleon was losing the war:
   - **Source C** shows him surrounded by enemies/looking worried/being savaged
   - **Source D** says Napoleon was defeated at Leipzig

History General Level—2002 (cont.)

4. (continued)

sources agree that Napoleon had many enemies:
- **Source C** shows him attacked by Britain, Austria, Russia
- **Source D** says Austrians, Prussians, Russians and Swedes attacked

sources agree that Austrians and Russians were against him:
- **Source C** shows the Austrian eagle and the Russian bear
- **Source D** says the Austrians and Russians attacked

Only **Source D** mentions Prussia and Sweden as part of the coalition

Only **Source C** shows Britain as part of the coalition.

5. The candidate evaluates the completeness of the explanation for the success of the Fourth Coalition using **presented evidence** such as:
- Austrians, Prussians, Russians and Swedes fought as allies against France
- Allies won the Battle of the Nations
- Napoleon and the French were forced to retreat back across the Rhine

and from **recalled evidence** such as:
- Napoleon not defeated until France was invaded in 1814
- role of British army: Peninsular War
- role of British naval blockade
- role of British economic strength eg financing coalitions

Unit II—Context B: 1890s–1920s
Section A

1. The candidate explains why the assassinations led to an outbreak of war using **presented evidence** such as:
- Archduke Franz Ferdinand was heir to the Austrian throne
- assassinations blamed on Serbia
- assassinations used as excuse to crush Serbian nationalism
- Bosnian desire for independence was a cause of tension

and **recalled evidence** such as:
- Austria-Hungary issued an ultimatum to Serbia
- Serbia refused the ultimatum
- Russia mobilised in support of Serbia
- Germany encouraged Austria-Hungary
- Austria-Hungary declared war on Russia
- Germany declared war on Russia and France
- the Alliance System in action
- Russia declared war on Austria-Hungary and Germany
- Britain is brought in on invasion of Belgium

2. The candidate assess the importance of rationing for British civilians using **presented evidence** such as:
- no problem; did more good than harm
- nation's health actually improved
- caused little hardship
- nation never faced with a famine

and **recalled evidence** such as:
- rationing restricted food supplies
- ration books had to be issued

2. (continued)
- by 1918 several commodities were rationed: butter, meat, sugar, margarine
- bread was never rationed
- rations were quite generous: provided a regular and sufficient food supply
- rationing was popular: seen as a fair method
- severe fines were imposed for breaching rationing
- Black Market
- queuing was lessened
- rationing in Germany was more severe
- other problems were more serious: air raids
- DORA and Total War affected more people
- casualty lists were a bigger problem
- panic buying and hoarding did occur

Section B

3. The candidate evaluates the usefulness of **Source C** using evidence such as:

contemporaneity:	taken at the time when tanks were being first used
authorship:	(official) photograph from Imperial War Museum (reputable) collection
content:	detail of tank (in action)
accuracy:	actual photograph/possibility of it being posed/taken in England
purpose:	to show a tank in action/to support the use of the tank
limitation:	omits detail on effectiveness: crew; speed; full weaponry; fascines etc

4. The candidate assesses agreement between **Sources C** and **D** with reference to evidence such as:

sources agree on use of method of propulsion/movement:
- **Source C** shows caterpillar tracks
- **Source D** refers to caterpillar tracks

sources agree about armour protection:
- **Source C** shows plate armour sheathing
- **Source D** refers to steel armour

sources agree about weapons:
- **Source C** shows machine guns
- **Source D** says "four machine guns"

sources agree tanks were used against barbed wire:
- **Source C** shows tanks coming up against barbed wire
- **Source D** says "used against entanglements of barbed wire"

Only **Source D** mentions speed; impossible to detect in **Source C**

Only **Source D** mentions crew of eight: cannot detect in **Source C**

Only **Source D** mentions problems—although there could be a problem in **Source C** as tank encounters thick wire

5. The candidate evaluates the completeness of the source with reference to **presented evidence** such as:
- tanks got stuck in mud
- (male) tanks used 6 pounder guns
- tanks could knock out pill boxes (concrete emplacements)
- tanks saved soldiers' lives

5. (continued)
- tanks could kill large numbers of enemy soldiers

and from **recalled evidence** such as:
- tanks were used against obstacles: fortifications; barbed wire
- tanks were often inefficient: broke down; tracks incapacitated
- tanks often broke telephone lines
- tank crews experienced problems
- tanks were relatively unsuccessful in early battles: eg Somme
- some initial success at Cambria but not sustained
- tanks were successful in later battles: eg Amiens

Unit II—Context C: 1930s–1960s
Section A
1. The candidate explains the reasons why Germany attacked Poland in September 1939 using **presented evidence** such as:
   - people of Danzig were mainly German
   - Danzig was separated from Germany by the Polish corridor
   - Hitler demanded Western Poland
   - Poles refused to give in to Hitler's demands (over Danzig)

   and **recalled evidence** such as:
   - land taken away at Versailles
   - Danzig was a free city created by the League
   - Danzig was a key port on the Baltic Sea
   - Polish Corridor had a high German population
   - Polish Corridor separated off East Prussia
   - Lebensraum

2. The candidate explains the importance of the 1961 Berlin Crisis using **presented evidence** such as:
   - Khrushchev tried to dominate Kennedy
   - America prepared for War
   - Soviets built Berlin Wall in revenge
   - US refusal to accept East Germany

   and **recalled evidence** such as:
   - Berlin became focus for Cold War
   - growing East–West suspicions
   - heightened tensions
   - fear of nuclear war
   - border was heavily defended
   - reasons for building the Wall

Section B
3. The candidate evaluates the usefulness of **Source C** using evidence such as:
   - contemporaneity: from period of air raid bombings
   - authorship: (respected) Scottish newspaper
   - content: describes after effects of an air raid
   - accuracy: no apparent exaggeration or bias: fits other evidence
   - limitation: only one air raid/on one district of Clydeside/only deals with effects on property not people

4. The candidate compares the evidence about the effects of an air raid with reference to evidence such as:

   sources agree on the wreckage:
   - **Source C**: broken glass, rubble, debris
   - **Source D**: shows rubble and wreckage

4. (continued)
sources agree that people recovered possessions:
- **Source C**: people returning to recover property
- **Source D** shows people removing possessions (a pram)

sources agree shops were destroyed:
- **Source C**: glass out of shop windows
- **Source D**: shows damaged shops (large windows; advertising hoardings)

sources agree homes destroyed:
- **Source C**: homes were ruined
- **Source D**: shows ruined homes (removal of domestic property)

sources differ in scale of destruction:
- **Source C**: says whole of district affected
- **Source D**: only shows one small area of one street

5. The candidate evaluates the completeness of **Source E** using **presented evidence** such as:
   - only one account (by a Scottish girl)
   - air raid siren sounded
   - plane could be heard
   - people panicked
   - bombs fell

   and from **recalled evidence** such as:
   - sometimes no warning
   - anti-aircraft guns fired
   - often many planes involved
   - people ran into shelters: Andersons; communal
   - carrying/wearing gas masks
   - time and extent of raids varied
   - morale of the civilians

Unit III—Context A: USA 1850–1880
Section A
1. The candidate describes the effects of the railroads on the West using **presented evidence** such as:
   - thousands of farms established
   - numbers of homesteaders increased
   - ranching and cattle trade benefited
   - animals transported
   - cities grew

   and **recalled evidence** such as:
   - railroads opened up the West
   - caused conflict with native Americans (Indians)
   - West became more law abiding
   - cattle taken to Chicago and the East
   - goods could be transported easily
   - cities like Dallas and Los Angeles grew
   - railroads supplied good transport

2. The candidate explains why Southerners were angry with Northerners using **presented evidence** such as:
   - had stolen Southern property
   - had murdered Southerners
   - had ignored the Supreme Court
   - had elected Lincoln as President

History General Level—2002 (cont.)

2. (continued)

and **recalled evidence** such as:
- angry at the North accepting runaway slaves
- concerned over tariff reform
- afraid that Lincoln will stop slavery in the New Territories
- afraid that Lincoln will abolish slavery
- concerned over state rights
- anger at compromise of 1850/free state status of California
- actions of abolitionists
- Harper's Ferry Raid

Section B

3. The candidate evaluates the attitude of Red Cloud in **Source C** using evidence such as:
- believes government wants to steal Indian territory
- thinks the government are trying to trick "Indians" into selling the land
- thinks native Americans are not being given enough time to decide
- he is not going to talk about it anymore
- he is ready to fight
- Red Cloud hates the US government

4. The candidate evaluates the degree of agreement between **Sources C** and **D** with reference to evidence such as:

sources agree the Bozeman Trail was a cause of conflict:
- **Source C**: come to steal the Bozeman Trail
- **Source D**: Sioux attacked soldiers on the Bozeman Trail

sources agree that the US army was involved:
- **Source C**: White Chief comes with soldiers
- **Source D**: US government intending to build forts

sources agree that the conflict involves violence (fighting):
- **Source C**: I will go now and fight you
- **Source D**: after much fighting between US Army and Sioux

sources agree that hunting was threatened:
- **Source C**: I will fight for the last hunting grounds
- **Source D**: Sioux feared for destruction of buffalo herds

Unit III—Context B: India 1917–1947
Section A

1. The candidate explains why life was unpleasant for Untouchables using **presented evidence** such as:
- they were regarded as outcasts
- they had to do tasks other Hindus would not do
- they were regarded as being below the caste system
- even their shadows were thought to contaminate

and **recalled evidence** such as:
- they were regarded as being beneath Brahmans, Kshatriyas, Vaisyas and Sudras
- they were forced into unpleasant jobs
- they became street sweepers, scavengers etc
- they were forbidden from mixed marriages
- they could not touch or be touched by others
- they lived in "outcast" areas of the town
- they could not enter a Hindu temple

2. The candidate describes the different views of Gandhi held by Indians using **presented evidence** such as:
- some did not like his love of Untouchables
- some thought he was Mahatma (a holy man)
- some asked for his blessing
- some were happy just to touch his feet
- some kissed the ground where he passed

and **recalled evidence** such as:
- some did not like the fact he called Untouchables "Harijans"—children of God
- some objected to his employing Untouchables
- some did not like the fact he adopted an Untouchable daughter
- some called him "the Great Soul"
- some thought him a great spiritual leader
- some admired his passive resistance methods (Satyagraha)
- some approved of his resistance to the Salt Laws
- some praised his reconciliation/pacifying actions in 1947
- some saw him as the man who brought independence
- some Hindus did not like his protection of the Muslim community
- some displaced Hindus disliked him
- many were horrified at his assassination

Section B

3. The candidate assesses the attitudes of the author of the Hunter Report in **Source C** using evidence such as:
- General Dyer acted hastily (as soon as he arrived)
- Dyer gave no warning to the crowd
- Dyer did not investigate what the meeting was about
- Dyer fired on an unarmed crowd
- unnecessary force was used
- Dyer treated the crowd as an easy target

4. The candidate assesses agreement between **Sources C** and **D** in terms of evidence such as:

sources agree that Dyer acted immediately:
- **Source C** says "as soon as General Dyer arrived"
- **Source D** says "immediately" went into action

sources agree that no warning was given to the crowd:
- **Source C** says "without giving the crowd any warning"
- **Source D** says "no warning was given"

sources agree that the crowd was unarmed:
- **Source C** says "None of them had any firearms"
- **Source D** says "the defenceless crowd"

sources agree that a lot of bullets were fired:
- **Source C** says "The soldiers fired 1,650 rounds of ammunition"
- **Source D** says the soldiers "ran out of ammunition"

Only **Source D** gives the scale of killing: 379 dead

Unit III—Context C: Russia 1914–1941
Section A

1. The candidate describes the main events of the February Revolution using **presented evidence** such as:
- demonstrations in Petrograd
- protests against food shortages
- factory workers went on strike
- troops mutinied

1. (continued)

and **recalled evidence** such as:
- detail of food protests, attacks on bakeries
- International Women's Day demonstration
- no public transport or newspapers
- detail on attitude of soldiers
- collapse of Petrograd garrison: soldiers join crowds
- formation of Provisional Government
- formation of Petrograd Soviet
- abdication of Nicholas II
- protest against other shortages, eg fuel
- involvement of the police
- involvement of students
- demonstrations/riots in Moscow

2. The candidate explains kulak opposition to collectivisation using **presented evidence** such as:
   - kulaks had to give up their land
   - kulaks had to give up their animals
   - kulaks had to give up tools
   - kulaks had to give up farm buildings
   - everything had to be divided up

   and **recalled evidence** such as:
   - kulaks had to give up their farm equipment
   - Stalin had said he wanted to destroy the kulaks
   - kulaks would no longer be able to hire people to work for them
   - kulaks were forced to join collectives
   - kulaks were often arrested, deported and executed
   - kulaks would lose identity/status/pride

Section B

3. The candidate identifies the attitude of Bukharin in **Source C** towards the opponents of Bolshevism using evidence such as:
   - should not be allowed freedom
   - not allowed freedom of press
   - not allowed freedom of speech
   - are enemies of the people
   - must be ruthlessly put down
   - must not be allowed back into power
   - only Bolsheviks should be in charge

4. The candidate assesses the degree of agreement between **Sources C** and **D** with reference to evidence such as:

   sources agree the Bolsheviks are ruthless:
   - **Source C:** we must ruthlessly put down our opponents
   - **Source D:** the Bolsheviks are ruthless

   sources agree that Bolshevik methods are not fair:
   - **Source C:** there can be no question of freedom/free press/free speech
   - **Source D:** the acts of the Bolsheviks are criminal

   sources agree that opponents of the Bolsheviks are not being allowed back into power:
   - **Source C:** must put down attempts of opponents to return to power
   - **Source D:** Bolsheviks preventing the return to power (of Provisional Government)

   sources disagree about law and order:
   - **Source C:** Bolsheviks are maintaining order
   - **Source D:** until the restoration of (law and) order

   sources disagree about who is in charge:
   - **Source C:** Party puts down opponents; we alone maintain order
   - **Source D:** I have taken on power, myself

4. (continued)

sources disagree about opposition to Bolsheviks:
- **Source C:** calls them "enemies of the people"
- **Source D:** wants the return of the Provisional Government

Unit III—Context D: Germany 1918–1939

Section A

1. The candidate describes the problems caused by hyperinflation using **presented evidence** such as:
   - children went hungry
   - children went short of clothing
   - there was terrible poverty
   - there was a decline in hygiene (cleanliness)
   - people suffered from cold

   and **recalled evidence** such as:
   - prices rose rapidly
   - money lost its value
   - workers wages rose more slowly than prices
   - savings became worthless
   - pensions lost value
   - bartering became commonplace

2. The candidate explains why Hitler was so popular using **presented evidence** such as:
   - he was successful
   - he provided strong leadership
   - he replaced weak, divided government
   - his rallies impressed people
   - he created an impression of confidence/purpose

   and **recalled evidence** such as:
   - his control of mass media
   - use of propaganda
   - control of the young
   - success of Olympic Games in 1936
   - achieved economic recovery
   - offered employment
   - restored Germany's reputation as a world power
   - other details of foreign policy
   - through "Strength through Joy" campaign
   - restored German pride

Section B

3. The candidate identifies Hitler's attitudes towards the Jews using evidence such as:
   - he hated them
   - accuses them of being robbers
   - he claims they have destroyed many civilisations
   - says they have not created anything worthwhile
   - accuses them of stealing art from others
   - accuses them of copying other peoples ideas

4. The candidate compares **Sources C** and **D** using evidence such as:

   sources agree that Hitler dislikes Jews:
   - **Source C:** Jews are a people of robbers
   - **Source D:** he argued they were lazy

   sources agree that Hitler thought the Jews have not done much of value:
   - **Source C:** have created nothing of their own
   - **Source D:** have contributed little

   sources agree the Jews have done little for civilisation:
   - **Source C:** they have never founded civilisation
   - **Source D:** had contributed little to world civilisation

   Only **Source C** says Hitler thought Jews destroyed civilisations

   Only **Source C** accuses them of stealing/copying

History General Level—2002 (cont.)

4. (continued)
   Only **Source D** says Hitler accused Jews of threatening Aryan supremacy

   Only **Source D** says Hitler blamed them for Germany losing First World War

   Only **Source D** says Hitler accused them for creating everything he disliked

History General Level—2003

Unit 1: Context A: 1750s – 1850s
Section A

1. The candidate describes working conditions in a cotton mill using **presented evidence** such as:
   - use of machinery
   - machines kept running
   - long hours of labour
   - some night work
   - working for six days a week
   - strictly supervised

   and **recalled evidence** such as:
   - factories were often grim
   - machinery was noisy and dangerous
   - accidents were frequent
   - factories had many health hazards
   - workers could be punished/beaten/fined
   - working in a mill was tiring
   - child labour brought problems
   - very low wages
   - lack of ventilation/hot dusty environment

2. The candidate assesses the importance of poor Lowland housing using **presented evidence** such as:
   - cottages were just hovels (huts/shacks)
   - interiors were dark and smoky
   - houses were built of stone and turf
   - houses had earth/dirt floors
   - chimney was just a hole in the roof
   - rain and snow could enter

   and **recalled evidence** such as:
   - windows were small and often unglazed
   - cooking was done on an open fire in middle of room
   - rooms were few and small
   - accommodation often shared with animals
   - box beds (often food stored underneath)
   - sanitation was poor/non-existent
   - bad ventilation
   - cold, damp conditions
   - overcrowding spread disease

   BUT
   - not all Lowland housing was poor
   - Improvers built substantial houses
   - other factors affected farming families

Section B

3. The candidate evaluates the usefulness of Source C using evidence such as:
   - <u>contemporaneity</u>:
     primary source written at the time (when Clearances happened)

3. (continued)
   - <u>authorship</u>:
     eyewitness account: estate manager with first hand experience
   - <u>content</u>:
     detail on benefits of Clearances
   - <u>accuracy</u>:
     may be backed up/contradicted by candidate evidence
   - <u>purpose</u>:
     to defend the Clearances/to inform of benefits
   - <u>limitation</u>:
     was his job to evict so obvious bias/just his view

4. The candidate selects evidence from **Source C** for the issue such as:
   - newly built fishermen's cottages for the evicted
   - weaving their nets around the fire (working in comfort)
   - contrast with previous poverty
   - contrast it with the previous filth
   - contrast it with a turf hut (of an unevicted tenant)
   - Highlanders not harmed by civilisation
   - Highlanders are well off

   The candidate selects evidence from **Source D** against the issue such as:
   - they were all on one day to quit (short notice of eviction)
   - given a few miserable patches of ground
   - without....the poorest hut to shelter them
   - great majority had never set foot in a boat (no clue about fishing)

5. The candidate suggests a conclusion to the issue using evidence as presented in Question 4 and relevant recalled evidence such as:

   for the issue:
   - some factors took time to explain the resettlement
   - evicted tenants lived together as a community
   - children could go to school
   - migration/emigration offered opportunities
   - some landlords provided alternative occupations

   against the issue:
   - Clearances were carried out cruelly
   - little time given for the removal of property
   - cottages set on fire
   - much distress and bitterness caused
   - many forced to migrate or emigrate
   - Highlands depopulated

UNIT I – Context B: 1830s – 1930s
Section A

1. The candidate describes changes in farming using **presented evidence** such as:
   - little ground wasted
   - all fields planted out
   - fields well planned/laid out
   - threshing done by steam power/machinery
   - steam power used

   and **recalled evidence** such as:
   - steam ploughs were used
   - new breeds of heavy horses used
   - machinery replaced hand labour
   - rural workers left to find work in towns
   - new machinery could lead to accidents
   - farm labourers' wages increased

2. The candidate assesses the importance of improvements made to rural housing using **presented evidence** such as:
   - solid stone or brick cottages constructed on most farms
   - floors of wood or stone were built
   - had fireplaces
   - running water being installed

   and **recalled evidence** such as:
   - kitchen equipment/ranges were also improving
   - many rural dwellings were still primitive
   - few still had indoor/flush toilets
   - lighting was still oil based
   - landlords were rebuilding cottages on their land

Section B
3. The candidate evaluates the usefulness of **Source C** using evidence such as:
   - contemporaneity:
     primary source written at the time (of 19th century emigration)
   - authorship:
     written by an actual emigrant/eyewitness
   - content:
     detail of experiences of emigration
   - accuracy:
     matched by other accounts
   - purpose:
     to encourage others to emigrate
   - bias/exaggeration:
     one-sided view/pro-emigration to Australia

4. The candidate identifies evidence for the issue using evidence from **Source C** such as:
   - it's encouraging others: tell all to come here
   - people will not starve as they do in Scotland
   - good wages: £10 a week paid
   - hopes of even better wages: £12 a week
   - independence can be gained
   - hard workers will do well

   The candidate identifies evidence against the issue from **Source D** such as:
   - daughter earns only £10 a year
   - dangerous jobs exist (for young women)
   - work in a flour mill is dangerous
   - low wages: 50p a week
   - long hours are worked: 14 a day
   - everyone wants it to rain/drought conditions
   - country not as good as made out to be

5. The candidate suggests a conclusion to the issue using evidence as presented in Question 4 and relevant recalled evidence such as:

   for the issue:
   - agents from Australia and Canada, promised better conditions
   - many Scots became successful farmers/businessmen/doctors etc
   - land was cheap
   - housing was available and cheaper than in Scotland
   - many Scots became influential figures abroad

   against the issue:
   - passage overseas was often long and hazardous and emigrants took ill

5. (continued)
   - some had little money and faced a difficult task of survival
   - some Scots did not settle and returned home
   - some Scots missed family and friends
   - some Scots disliked the weather/snakes/insects

UNIT I – Context C: 1880s to the Present Day
Section A
1. The candidate describes the ways trade unions changed in the early 20th century using **presented evidence** such as:
   - better organised
   - many more unions
   - smaller unions joined larger ones
   - Scottish and English unions joined

   and **recalled evidence** such as:
   - unskilled unions formed
   - women joined unions
   - women formed their own unions
   - union membership increased
   - unions became more powerful
   - industrial action increased
   - unions became involved in politics
   - unions helped create the Labour Party

2. The candidate assesses how serious (important) a problem poor rural housing was in the early 20th century using **presented evidence** such as:
   - no piped water supply
   - rain/well water was used
   - no indoor sanitation
   - no outdoor toilets: hillside/quarry used
   - no bath (room)/primitive bathing facilities

   and **recalled evidence** such as:
   - some houses still had earth floors
   - no chimneys – smoky interiors
   - dampness
   - thatched roof/no ceilings
   - lack of electricity
   - bothies were primitive
   - black houses still existed

   BUT
   some improvements eg
   - stone/wood floors
   - slate roofs
   - running water
   - proper sanitation
   - electricity being installed

Section B
3. The candidate evaluates the usefulness of **Source C** using evidence such as:
   - contemporaneity:
     primary source written at the time (of the period of emigration)
   - authorship:
     journalist/someone who has researched
   - content:
     details of hardships in Fraserburgh/Scotland
   - limitation:
     one person's opinion/only Fraserburgh
   - consistency:
     agrees with other opinions/evidence

History General Level—2003 (cont.)

3. (continued)
- purpose:
  to inform readers what was happening in the area

4. The candidate selects evidence for the issue from **Source C** such as:
   - long queues of (unemployed) at Labour Exchanges
   - many poor, able-bodied men
   - many on poor relief/getting help from Parish Poor Fund
   - Fraserburgh has not been flourishing
   - there were 'bad times'
   - steady stream of young in search of livelihood

   The candidate selects other factors from **Source D** such as:
   - because they were pulled, not pushed
   - cheap farmland available
   - lots of employment opportunities
   - hopes of becoming rich
   - skilled jobs available abroad

5. The candidate suggests a conclusion to the issue using presented evidence as given in Question 4 and relevant recalled evidence such as:

   For the issue:
   - many could not make a living from farming/crofting
   - slumps in industry caused unemployment
   - living conditions were poor
   - wages were low
   - could not afford higher rents (eg in Highlands)

   Other reasons:
   - driven out by Highland Clearances
   - join relatives already abroad
   - search for a challenge/adventure
   - search for a better way of life
   - encouragement/incentives offered by countries abroad

UNIT II – Context A: 1790s – 1820s
Section A

1. The candidate explains the ways in which the Edict of Fraternity contributed to the outbreak of war using **presented evidence** such as:
   - Edict called on people to overthrow their rulers
   - French had overthrown their ruler
   - British government became colder towards France

   and **recalled evidence** such as:
   - French had imprisoned Louis XVI
   - soon after (Jan 1793) King Louis was executed
   - Edict called on people to rebel (have a revolution)
   - Government/monarchy was alarmed at possible revolution in Britain
   - War was declared on February 1st, 1793
   - other issues brought war close:
     - violence and bloodshed in France
     - opening of River Scheldt
     - risk of invasion

2. The candidate describes life in the navy using **presented evidence** such as:
   - some sailors were press-ganged
   - conditions were better in the merchant navy
   - wages were low in the navy (better in merchant navy)

2. (continued)
   - sailors often were not allowed to leave their ship
   - some sailors might disagree with the captain

   and from **recalled evidence** such as:
   - food was poor
   - ships biscuits often affected by weevils/maggots
   - water supplies were often polluted
   - scurvy often occurred
   - punishment was severe eg flogging; keel-hauling; hanging
   - sleeping arrangements were primitive
   - sailors were often commanded by young midshipmen
   - prize money could be gained

Section B

3. The candidate determines the attitudes towards the Congress of Vienna expressed in Source C using evidence such as:
   - it did not redraw the map of Europe for ever
   - it reflected the wishes of the great powers
   - it ignored national hopes of many
   - it ignored nationalistic desires of Italians and Belgians
   - it led to trouble in the future
   - it was praiseworthy in not treating France too harshly

4. The candidate assesses the degree of agreement between **Sources C and D** using evidence such as:

   Sources agree that the Congress was not satisfactory
   - Source C says: led to trouble in the future
   - Source D says: there were criticisms of the treaty

   Sources agree that the Congress ignored principle of nationalism
   - Source C says: ignored the national hopes of many
   - Source D says: ignored the principle of nationalism

   Sources agree that the wishes of the Belgians were not listened to
   - Source C says: ignored the (national) hopes of the Belgians
   - Source D says: the people of Belgium were placed under the Dutch

   Sources agree that the national hopes of the Italians were ignored
   - Source C says: ignored (national) hopes of Italians
   - Source D says: Italians were put under Austrians

   Sources agree that Congress suited the wishes of the great powers
   - Source C says: reflected wishes of great powers
   - Source D says: to suit wishes of great powers

   Sources disagree about main success of Congress
   - Source C says: praised for not defeating France too harshly
   - Source D says: major success was no war till 1854

UNIT II – Context B: 1890s – 1920s
Section A

1. The candidate explains the reasons for tension in the Balkans using **presented evidence** such as:
   - Different nationalities were mixed together
   - Austria and Russia both wanted to control the region

1. (continued)
- Austria and Russia both wanted Mediterranean access through the Balkans

and **recalled evidence** such as:
- power vacuum caused by decline of Turkey
- disputes between Balkan countries and Turkey
- disputes between Balkan countries themselves
- details of Bosnian crisis 1908
- Balkan Wars of 1912/1913
- Austrian-Serbian rivalry
- activities of the Black Hand

2. The candidate describes conditions for soldiers on the Western Front using **presented evidence** such as:
   - trenches were knee-deep in mud
   - soldiers drowned in shell holes
   - flooding was a problem
   - frostbite was common in cold weather

   and **recalled evidence** such as:
   - lice were a problem
   - existence of rats
   - monotonous food (bully beef, rations)
   - enemy snipers
   - artillery/machine gun firing
   - gas attacks
   - shell shock
   - heat/flies in summer
   - trench foot

Section B
3. The candidate discusses Clemenceau's attitude towards Germans using evidence such as:
   - does not have a high opinion of them
   - they only understand fear/threats
   - thinks they were merciless
   - says you cannot talk to them/never negotiate with them
   - says you must not compromise with them
   - says you must dictate to them (or lose respect)

   and possible **recalled evidence** such as:
   - Clemenceau hostile to Germans
   - angry as had twice seen his country invaded
   - was called 'The Tiger' as he was aggressive towards Germans

4. The candidate assesses agreement/disagreement between the sources using evidence such as:

   Sources agree that Germans were aggressive
   - Source C says: only understand threats/aggressive action
   - Source D says: most aggressive people

   Sources agree that the Germans are merciless/aggressive
   - Source C says: they are without mercy
   - Source D says: they react violently

   Sources disagree about how to treat Germans
   - Source C says: must never negotiate with them/must dictate to them
   - Source D says: should not treat them as underdogs

4. (continued)
Sources disagree about results of threatening Germans
- Source C says: must dictate or no respect shown
- Source D says: Germans will react strongly to injustice

Only Source D says they are civilised

UNIT II – Context C: 1930s – 1960s
Section A
1. The candidate explains the consequences of the Munich Crisis using **presented evidence** such as:
   - Peace was not obtained
   - Germany pressurised the Poles
   - Germans demanded the return of Danzig
   - Hitler stepped up pressure on Czechoslovakia

   and **recalled evidence** such as:
   - Hitler got what he wanted at Munich (without fighting)
   - Hitler's prestige and ambitions increased
   - Western powers made to look weak
   - Czechs no longer trusted Britain and France
   - Czechs and Slovaks were bullied
   - Slovaks encouraged to declare independence
   - Hitler invaded all Czechoslovakia
   - Hitler got time to prepare for war
   - Britain and France realised that Hitler could not be trusted
   - Germany eventually attacked Poland

2. The candidate describes the effects of the atomic bomb on Japanese civilians using **presented evidence** such as:
   - made people flee from the city
   - badly burned people
   - caused skin to hang off/peel away
   - faces and hands swollen

   and **recalled evidence** such as:
   - killed thousands
   - injured 70,000
   - widespread fires burned people
   - radiation sickness
   - caused terrible symptoms: vomiting; hair falling out
   - made thousands homeless
   - caused children to be born with physical defects
   - caused collapse of civilian morale
   - contribution towards ending the war

Section B
3. The candidate evaluates the attitude of Patrick Rooke towards the UN using evidence such as:
   - is very positive about it/has a high opinion of it
   - acknowledges there have been doubts about it
   - believes it has proved its worth
   - says it has not stopped war/minor wars continued
   - thinks it has stopped small wars becoming great conflicts
   - credits it with maintaining general peace
   - believes it is firmly established

4. The candidate assesses agreement between Sources C and D using evidence such as:

   Sources agree UN has been a success
   - Source C says: has proved its value
   - Source D says: hopes and plans largely achieved

History General Level—2003 (cont.)

4. (continued)
Sources agree it has maintained the peace
- Source C says: general peace has been maintained
- Source D says: no large scale war has threatened peace

Sources agree that UN has had to deal with threats to world peace:
- Source C says: have been a number of localised wars
- Source D says: have been tensions between nations

Only Source C mentions doubts about the UN

Only Source C claims it is firmly established

Only Source D mentions the development work of UN organisations

UNIT III – Context A: USA 1850 – 1880
Section A
1. The candidate explains the effects of westward expansion on the native Americans using **presented evidence** such as:
   - buffalo getting fewer
   - nomadic tribes broken up
   - alcohol abuse becoming a problem
   - military presence subduing them

   and from **recalled evidence** such as:
   - buffalo almost driven to extinction
   - reliance on the buffalo for all needs no longer possible
   - hunting grounds disturbed
   - loss of homeland
   - loss of freedom – removal to reservations
   - destruction of way of life/loss of culture
   - Whites regarded native Americans as inferior
   - decline of population
   - diseases brought by White settlers affected them
   - loss of power: tribes not seen as nations
   - increasing dependence on Whites

2. The candidate assesses the importance of the Union to Abraham Lincoln using **presented evidence** such as:
   - the Union is perpetual/will last forever
   - the Union cannot be destroyed
   - it is a contract made between states
   - it cannot be broken unless both sides want it
   - it is a revolutionary act for one state to act against the Union

   and from **recalled evidence** such as:
   - the American states should remain united
   - the United States is a national entity
   - the Union was created in 1774 by the Articles of Association
   - the Union was ratified in the 1776 Declaration of Independence
   - it is illegal to secede from the Union
   - Lincoln will do all in his power to preserve the Union
   - Lincoln does not want a Civil War to divide the Union

Section B
3. The candidate evaluates the usefulness of Source C using evidence such as:
   - <u>contemporaneity</u>:
     primary source produced at the time (of legal slavery)
   - <u>authorship</u>:
     written by a slave owner
   - <u>content</u>:
     detail on the practice of owning slaves: shows a runaway slave
   - <u>accuracy</u>:
     shows attitude of most slave owners: slaves as property
   - <u>purpose</u>:
     to persuade others to help recapture 'lost property'
   - <u>limitation</u>:
     doesn't show other horrors: punishment; use of dogs to hunt runaways

4. The candidate evaluates the opinions of Abolitionists using evidence such as:
   - condemn/accuse/blame slave owners
   - think supporters of slavery are sinners
   - believe slavery supporters should seek forgiveness
   - think it is cowardly not to oppose slavery

5. The candidate assesses the accuracy of Source E using **presented evidence** such as:
   - slavery was chief cause of the war
   - slavery was essential to Southern economy and should not be attacked
   - attacks on slavery has alarmed Southern states
   - opponents of slavery did not want it to expand
   - opponents of slavery did not want to compete against slave labour

   and **recalled evidence** such as:
   - Northern states were opposed to slavery
   - North was generally abolitionist
   - many Northerners against horrors of slave life
   - fears about destruction of Southern way of life
   - fears that slave-owning South was holding back industrial North
   - economic differences existed between North (industrial) and South (plantation)
   - disagreement about tariffs
   - secession: Southern states wanted to opt out of Union
   - Northern states determined to preserve Union
   - election of Lincoln seen as the last straw
   - leaders unwilling to compromise

UNIT III – Context B: India 1917 – 1947
Section A
1. The candidate explains reasons for Indian discontent with British rule using **presented evidence** such as:
   - it humiliated Indians
   - it hurt Indian pride
   - it made Indians feel like subjects of the British

   and **recalled evidence** such as:
   - use of British 'divide and rule' tactics
   - discrimination against Indians
   - Indians could not reach upper ranks of Indian Civil Service
   - Indians could not reach upper ranks of the army
   - repressive laws; eg Rowlett Act
   - violent repression; eg Amritsar Massacre

1. **(continued)**
   - economic exploitation
   - British wanted to take over their country
   - control of school/use of English language
   - suppression of 'native' culture

2. The candidate evaluates the importance of Nehru's role using **presented evidence** such as:
   - dedicated his life to the nationalist (independence) struggle
   - spent years in prison (a martyr for the cause)
   - broadened the appeal of Congress
   - maintained Congress unity
   - achieved independence
   - did not achieve a united India

   and **recalled evidence** such as:
   - less important than Gandhi
   - co-operated with Gandhi
   - negotiated with Mountbatten
   - accomplished independence in 1947
   - policies may have contributed to split with Muslim League
   - may have contributed to Partition

Section B

3. The candidate evaluates the usefulness of Source C using evidence such as:
   - <u>contemporaneity</u>:
     primary source produced at the time (of the Salt March)
   - <u>authorship</u>:
     photographic record clearly showing Gandhi on a protest march
   - <u>content</u>:
     shows Gandhi and followers protesting
   - <u>accuracy</u>:
     accurate depiction of Gandhi and his peaceful protests
   - <u>purpose</u>:
     newspaper usage: inform readership of actual happening
   - <u>limitation</u>:
     does not show scale of the march

4. The candidate evaluates Gandhi's attitude to cotton production using evidence such as:
   - wants to end India's dependence on England
   - says Indians should boycott cloth made in England
   - thinks it is the patriotic duty of Indians to make cotton
   - believes Indians should spin their own cotton in India
   - believes the self-production of cotton is an effective attack on England

5. The candidate evaluates the completeness of Source E using **presented evidence** such as:
   - Gandhi went all over India
   - preached non-co-operation
   - said to boycott British cloth
   - urged Indians to stop wearing foreign clothing
   - advocated civil disobedience

   and **recalled evidence** such as:
   - urged people to break the law
   - urged non-violent, Satyagraha, passive resistance methods
   - encouraged fasting
   - built up Indian National Congress

5. **(continued)**
   - hartal
   - attended conferences
   - met representatives of Britain
   - tried to overcome religious and class differences in India

UNIT III – Context C: Russia 1914 – 1941
Section A

1. The candidate explains why the Tsar was disliked using **presented evidence** such as:
   - he made all major decisions
   - ordinary Russians had no say
   - he alone was head of the army
   - he picked his own ministers
   - his advisors were all from the nobility

   and **recalled evidence** such as:
   - he was all powerful/an autocrat
   - interests of peasants and town workers ignored
   - use of the secret police
   - use of the army/Cossacks to crush unrest
   - censorship of books and newspapers
   - opponents exiled to Siberia
   - poor working conditions blamed on Tsar
   - mirs instructed what to do
   - the unpopularity of the Tsarina

2. The candidate assesses the importance of weak leadership as a factor explaining the defeat of the Whites using evidence such as:
   - Whites lacked a single leader in command/ generals jealous of each other
   - White generals did not co-operate (attack at the same time)
   - White generals were brutal and that put off possible supporters

   and from **recalled evidence** such as:
   - Reds had good leadership
   - Trotsky made the Red Army an efficient fighting unit
   - Trotsky travelled around the front line by train
   - Cheka enforced discipline
   - foreign intervention made Whites appear unpatriotic
   - Bolsheviks kept control of main cities

Section B

3. The candidate evaluates the attitude of the author towards the continuation of the war using evidence such as:
   - dislikes fighting in the war
   - wonders what the fighting is for
   - wants to fight for democracy – not capitalist success
   - willing to fight in defence of Revolution
   - doesn't like being forced to fight
   - wants to fight to give land to the peasants
   - wants to fight to give factories to the workers
   - wants to fight for something worthwhile
   - wants to fight to give power to the Soviets

4. The candidate evaluates the usefulness of Source C using evidence such as:
   - <u>contemporaneity</u>:
     primary source, taken at the time (when Provisional Government was in power)

History General Level—2003 (cont.)

4. (continued)
- <u>authorship</u>:
  photographic record clearly showing the hardship of women in the food queue
- <u>content</u>:
  shows hardship of women waiting for food
- <u>limitation</u>:
  only one part of one city/does not show actual starvation
- <u>purpose</u>:
  taken to record the suffering/used as propaganda?
- <u>accuracy</u>:
  reflects food shortage
  may be propaganda photograph and thus biased.

5. The candidate assesses the completeness of Source E with reference to **presented evidence** such as:
   - Lenin spent years preparing for revolution
   - Lenin realised the unpopularity of the war
   - Lenin formed a group of revolutionaries
   - Lenin's slogans appealed

   and **recalled evidence** such as:
   - Lenin ensured that he gained the support of the influential Petrograd Soviet.
   - Lenin promised Peace, Bread and Land
   - Trotsky also did much of the planning
   - role of the Red Guard
   - failures of the Provisional Government

UNIT III – Context D: Germany 1918 – 1939
Section A

1. The candidate explains why many Germans were unhappy with the Versailles Settlement using **presented evidence** such as:
   - were forced to accept the treaty
   - were punished by the treaty
   - had to live under foreign rule
   - Austria not allowed to join with Germany

   and **recalled evidence** such as:
   - were forced to accept War Guilt Clause
   - some Germans forced to live in Poland and Czechoslovakia
   - forced to pay Reparations
   - forced to accept the Diktat
   - had military terms imposed on them
   - lost colonies
   - lost land

2. The candidate explains the importance of Göbbels' propaganda work using **presented evidence** such as:
   - propaganda controlled all expression/communication
   - a **Ministry** of Propaganda shows its importance
   - propaganda spread the Nazi message
   - censorship was an important tool
   - Göbbels controlled the media

   BUT ALSO
   - opponents suffered (use of intimidation)

   and **recalled evidence** such as:
   - it highlighted Nazi strength eg at rallies (Nuremberg)
   - it influenced what people read in newspapers
   - it dominated radio and cinema
   - it encouraged loyalty

2. (continued)
   - it encouraged support/idolisation of Hitler
   - it encouraged anti-semitism
   - it played a vital part in Nazi rise to power

   BUT ALSO
   - use of force/intimidation
   - use of Gestapo/SS
   - concentration camps
   - popular support for Nazis: rallies etc

Section B

3. The candidate evaluates the usefulness of Source C using evidence such as:
   - <u>contemporaneity</u>:
     primary source, taken at the time (of the period of hyperinflation)
   - <u>authorship</u>:
     photographic evidence clearly showing an effect of hyperinflation
   - <u>content</u>:
     shows men needing a washing basket to carry wages
   - <u>consistency</u>:
     agrees with candidate's own knowledge of hyperinflation
   - <u>accuracy</u>:
     may be staged but looks accurate
   - <u>limitation</u>:
     does not show misery and despair of hyperinflation

4. The candidate identifies the attitudes of the author towards political parties using evidence such as:
   - prefers National Socialist party
   - hates parties who support/use parliamentary politics/democracy
   - against the higgling and haggling (derogatory language) of parties
   - hates coalitions
   - hates the confusion parties are in
   - thinks other political parties are full of rascals
   - wants to throw other parties out

5. The candidate assesses the completeness of the source using **presented evidence** such as:
   - blamed Weimar for increase in unemployment
   - blamed Weimar for making people stand in long dole queues
   - found Hitler's promises more attractive
   - blamed for immediate effects of Wall Street Crash

   and from **recalled evidence** such as:
   - blamed them for not coping with the Depression following the Wall Street Crash
   - still remembered previous period of hyperinflation
   - still blamed them for ending the war/signing Versailles
   - were disillusioned with democracy
   - feared growth of Communism

Marking at Credit Level

Marks should be awarded to the candidate for:
carrying out the correct process
using relevant recalled evidence
using relevant presented evidence (in Section B, Enquiry Skills, only)

In Section B any item which requires the use of relevant recall is clearly indicated and full marks can only be awarded to these items when such recall is used.

Section A (Knowledge and Understanding)
All questions are based on recalled evidence. A *selection* of possible recall is given in the Marking Instructions. The marker will use professional judgement to determine the relevance of other possible recall.

In a K3 answer (assessing the importance) the candidate should be credited for either explaining the importance of the presented factor and/or by assessing the relative importance of relevant recalled evidence. In both cases a judgement should be offered.

Section B (Enquiry Skills)
NB: At Credit Level, process in itself is not rewarded.

In an ES1 item in Unit I it is not enough to say that a source is useful because it deals with the issue/investigation under discussion. The evaluation must make specific reference to the actual source/s as in all ES1 type items.

Examples:

This source is useful as it was written during a period of great changes in farming in the late 18th century   = 1 mark

This source is useful as it was written by a reputable historian who will have studied the relevant primary sources
= 1 mark

This source is useful as it was written at the time (of the investigation)   = 0 marks

This source is reliable as it was written by a man living then (at the time)   = 0 marks

This source is valuable as it was written during the period under investigation   = 0 marks

In Unit I, in an ES1 item, if a candidate makes references to the usefulness of the content of each of the two sources a maximum of 2 marks can be awarded.

If a candidate makes an accurate evaluation which relates to both sources 2 marks can be awarded.

Examples:

These sources are useful as they are both eye witness accounts   = 2 marks

These sources are useful as they were written at both ends of the time period we are studying and allow us to compare changes from 1830–1930   = 2 marks

In all other ES1 questions, in Units II and III, only 1 mark can be awarded for an accurate evaluation of content.

In an ES2 question 1 mark is given for a simple comparison and 2 marks for a developed point. Examples are given in the Marking Instructions.

In an ES4 item, which asks the candidate to put a source into its historical context, full marks cannot be awarded unless relevant recall is given.

In an ES5 item (Question 4 of Unit I) listing or copying of relevant evidence from the presented sources **is allowed** and should be **fully credited**.

Recall or personal judgement *cannot* be credited at all.

If evidence is selected on only one side of the given issue, the maximum obtainable is 3 marks.

In an ES6 item (Question 5 of Unit I) the candidate must:
use presented evidence
show relevant recall
show some balance of answer

If any of the above three requirements is not met, the maximum obtainable is 2 marks.

(NB: There is no need for a balanced conclusion as such but the answer must show balance.)

The 8 mark, extended response (in Unit I in the 2002 examination) must be correctly structured as an **essay: ie correctly addressing the detailed requirements of the item, in paragraphs, with an introduction and an appropriate conclusion. Marks will be deducted for any failure to satisfy these requirements**.

The abbreviations K1 – K3, and E1 – E6 used above indicate the particular sub skills of the extended EGRC to which an individual question relates:

K1: description; K2: explanation; K3: importance;
ES1: evaluation; ES2: comparison; ES3: point of view; ES4: set in context; ES5: select evidence; ES6: present conclusion.

History—Credit Level

INTRODUCTION

Knowledge and Understanding
Answers are given as bullet points. Candidates must always respond in full sentences, addressing the correct process and actually responding to the item: either describing, explaining or assessing importance (preferably with reference to other important factors).

In the 8 mark, extended writing exercise the candidate should structure the response appropriately with an introduction, six points of relevant, supporting evidence and a conclusion which clearly addresses the specific requirements of the item.

Enquiry Skills
Evaluation of evidence: normally, only 1 mark will be allocated <u>for each type</u> of evaluation offered: contemporaneity; authorship; content; purpose etc.
Comparing Sources: 1 mark is allocated for a simple comparison; 2 marks for a developed comparison. Examples of both types are given.
Assessing attitude: 1 mark is allocated for each assessment or explanation.
Putting a source in context: full marks can only be awarded if recall is used.
Selecting evidence to address an issue: this is the only area where a candidate can supply bullet points or list evidence.
Providing a conclusion: full marks cannot be awarded unless the candidate uses presented evidence + recall + balance in their response.

History Credit Level—2001

Unit I—Context A: 1750s–1850s

Section A

1. The candidate describes the technological changes in cotton production using evidence such as:
   - Kay's flying shuttle
   - Hargreaves' spinning jenny
   - Arkwright's water frame
   - Crompton's mule
   - Cartwright's power loom
   - automated carding machines
   - details on the use/techniques of the above
   - use of water power
   - use of steam power
   - use of mass production techniques

2. The candidate explains whether Scotland's urban housing problems were solved by building tenements using evidence such as:
   - there were not enough houses in urban areas
   - tenements were tall blocks of flats which supplied living space
   - many people could be accommodated in a small space
   - some tenement blocks were well looked after and supplied good conditions
   - some tenements were often built of cheap, inferior materials
   - overcrowding was often not solved; tenement dwelling was cramped
   - tenements were built in close proximity to each other
   - facilities often had to be shared
   - often one room dwelling/no bedrooms
   - disease was often prevalent
   - there was a lack of privacy
   - tenements often lacked sanitation or running water
   - tenements were sometimes wet and squalid
   - some tenants lived in unhygienic basements
   - provided accommodation near employment/factories

Section B

3. The candidate evaluates Sources A and B using evidence such as:

   Source A
   - authorship: from reputable historian—likely to be reliable
   - limitation: only one author's opinion "Radical war was pathetic"
   - content: describes the incident at Bonnymuir
   - accuracy: says three Bonnymuir radicals executed: in fact only two resulted from Bonnymuir; otherwise backed up by other evidence

   Source B
   - authorship: eyewitness/involved speaker
   - contemporaneity: primary source from time of Radical incident
   - accuracy: biased account—stating reasons for involvement
   - purpose: purpose is to excuse/account for involvement
   - content: describes one man's part in events

3. (continued)
   Both Sources:
   Two sides of the argument are given

4. The candidate identifies supporting evidence in the sources such as:

   Source A
   - events (Bonnymuir) caused alarm among authorities
   - newspapers covered the events (Bonnymuir)
   - discussions followed events (Bonnymuir)
   - later discussions contributed to political change
   - "left the authorities looking foolish"

   Source B
   - James Wilson lost his life for the cause
   - Wilson—a pioneering freedom fighter
   - Radical activity would help free country from political shame
   - Radical events will live in history

   Source C
   - a number of prisoners taken
   - three men were hanged (political martyrs)
   - Wilson's hanging was scandalous (aroused sympathy)
   - some men were transported (major event)
   - juries sympathised with accused men (won public support)

   The candidate identifies conflicting evidence in the sources such as:

   Source A:
   - Radical war was "pathetic"
   - Bonnymuir was a "minor skirmish"
   - authorities rather foolish at the alarm caused (a lot of fuss about nothing)

   Source B
   - the authorities are in control
   - Radicals were arrested and tried

   Source C
   - Bonnymuir was just a "short fight"
   - only four Radicals were wounded
   - only three Radicals executed
   - when standard of living improved agitation settled down
   - newspapers also helped in the fight for political reform (not just Radicals)

5. The candidate offers a conclusion on the issue and shows balance in the answer, using relevant presented evidence as outlined above and recalled evidence such as:

   For the issue:
   - aim of Bonnymuir was to capture weapons from Carron Iron Works
   - Government troops attacked Radicals at Bonnymuir
   - John Baird and Andrew Hardie were hanged
   - worry about mob riots
   - Wilson was involved in a radical march at Strathaven
   - 20,000 watched Wilson's death on Glasgow Green
   - all three who died became martyrs
   - 19 were transported to Australia (the Scottish Insurrectionists)
   - newspapers such as "The Scotsman" covered the event

5. (continued)
- Bonnymuir brought lack of working class freedoms to public notice

against the issue
- only a small group of Glasgow Radicals marched towards Carron Iron Works
- only 47 prisoners were taken at Bonnymuir
- authorities were alarmed but exaggerated the menace posed
- agents provocateurs exaggerated the events
- military power was always on top of events
- whole Radical War lasted just 5 days
- violence is not a great feature of Scottish working class protest
- other factors played a part in development of democracy
- peaceful protests: petitions; letters to newspapers etc played a part in change
- extension of the franchise came in 1832 (but not to everyone)

Unit I—Context B: 1830s–1930s

Section A

1. The candidate describes changes in coal mining as a result of new technology by 1930 using evidence such as:
   - electrical coal cutting equipment
   - electric lighting
   - safety lighting
   - steam and electrical power to raise cages
   - wagon ways
   - ventilation fans
   - metal or concrete pit props

2. The candidate explains the reasons why there was so much poor housing during the 19th century using evidence such as:
   - needs of workers to find accommodation
   - high rents/low wages
   - demand outstripped supply
   - many houses badly constructed (jerry built)
   - poor/cheap building materials used
   - housing often not looked after well
   - desire for quick profits
   - needs of industry to house workers/cause of overcrowding
   - population growth/movements and demand for housing
   - lack of central and local government control

Section B

3. The candidate evaluates the sources using evidence such as:

   Source A
   - authorship: a Suffragette—one converted to their cause
   - contemporaneity: speech at a Suffragette function in 1908
   - content: Suffragettes are getting attention
   - accuracy: supporter of the cause so likely bias
   - purpose: to win support for Suffragettes: show sympathy for the cause (said at Suffragette function)

   Source B
   - authorship: written by a modern historian who has researched the topic

3. (continued)
   - contemporaneity: secondary source with hindsight to events
   - content: says government not giving in to law breakers
   - limitation: one person's opinion: "law breaking" weakened case

   Together, the sources show both sides of the argument

4. The candidate selects evidence that the Suffragettes did harm the "votes for women" cause such as:

   Source A
   - Suffragettes created rows at Westminster: annoyed MPs: acted against them

   Source B
   - law breaking strengthened the argument that women could not be trusted/did not deserve the vote
   - government took a tough line against Suffragettes
   - Suffrage movement split

   Source C
   - many viewed militancy with disgust
   - many believed lawful/peaceful methods were better/more effective

   The candidate selects evidence that the Suffragettes did not harm the "vote for women" cause such as:

   Source A
   - nothing had been done more for the cause
   - cause brought to public attention
   - more done by Suffragettes than in previous 60 years
   - author has been convinced by Suffragette actions

   Source B
   - Suffragettes believed extreme actions would force the government's hand

   Source C
   - no attention paid to cause until 1905 when militancy began
   - militant tactics have drawn public attention

5. The candidate reaches a balanced conclusion using **presented evidence** such as:

   For the issue:
   - Government took a tough line against militancy
   - people did not trust women
   - methods not effective
   - Suffrage movement divided

   Against the issue
   - methods brought cause to attention of public and government
   - more done by Suffragettes than other groups

   and from **recalled evidence** such as:

   For the issue:
   - details of violence which disgusted people
   - anger at Suffragette outrages
   - Suffragettes arrested: Government hard line
   - Cat and Mouse Act

   Against the Issue:
   - public sympathy for brave Suffragettes (Hunger Strikers; martyr(s))
   - Cat and Mouse Act attracted sympathy
   - media attention
   - effect of women's war work

History Credit Level—2001 (cont.)

Unit I—Context C: 1880s–Present Day

Section A

1. The candidate describes how shipbuilding improved using evidence such as:
   - steam replaced sail
   - turbine engines used
   - diesel engines used
   - bodywork changed from wood to iron then steel
   - ship sections were welded not riveted
   - prefabrication techniques made better ships
   - computer-aided technology used to make ships
   - ship design improved
   - identical ships built to exact specifications
   - electric furnaces used
   - high-tech cranes
   - pneumatic riveters
   - indoor shipbuilding facilities

2. The candidate gives a balanced explanation of whether housing improved in Scotland using evidence such as:
   - council estates built
   - housing moved from city centre to pleasanter outskirts/suburbs
   - high rise flats built: good and bad points
   - prefabs built: good and bad points
   - housing estates could lack community spirit
   - estates experienced vandalism
   - estates often lacked amenities
   - new towns built in 50s and 60s
   - new towns often had good facilities
   - renovation of tenements (1980s)
   - increase in house ownership—houses well looked after
   - great deal of poor housing remained

Section B

3. The candidate evaluates the sources using evidence such as:

   Source A
   - authorship: a Suffragette—one converted to their cause
   - contemporaneity: speech at Suffragette function in 1908
   - content: Suffragettes are getting attention
   - accuracy: supporter of the cause so likely bias
   - purpose: to win support for Suffragettes: show sympathy for the cause (said at Suffragette function)

   Source B
   - authorship: written by a modern historian who has researched the topic
   - contemporaneity: secondary source with hindsight to events
   - content: says government not giving in to law breakers
   - accuracy: one person's opinion–"law breaking" weakened the case

   Together the sources show both sides of the argument

4. The candidate selects evidence that the Suffragettes did harm the "votes for women" cause such as:

   Source A
   - Suffragettes created rows at Westminster; annoyed MPs; acted against them

   Source B
   - law breaking strengthened the argument that women could not be trusted/did not deserve the vote
   - government took a tough line against Suffragettes
   - Suffrage movement split

   Source C
   - many viewed militancy with disgust
   - many believed peaceful/lawful methods were better/more effective

   The candidate selects evidence that the Suffragettes did not harm the "vote for women" cause such as:

   Source A
   - nothing had done more for the cause
   - cause brought to public attention
   - more done by Suffragettes than in previous 60 years
   - author has been convinced by Suffragette action

   Source B
   - Suffragettes believed extreme actions would force the government's hand

   Source C
   - no attention paid to cause until 1905 when militancy began
   - militant tactics have drawn public attention

5. The candidate reaches a balanced conclusion using **presented evidence** such as:

   For the issue:
   - Government took a tough line against militancy
   - people did not trust women
   - methods not effective
   - Suffrage movement divided

   Against the issue
   - methods brought cause to attention of public and government
   - more done by militant Suffragettes than other groups

   and from **recalled evidence** such as:

   For the Issue
   - details of violence which disgusted people
   - anger at Suffragette outrages
   - Suffragettes arrested: Government hard line
   - Cat and Mouse Act

   Against the issue:
   - public sympathy for brave Suffragettes (Hunger strikes; martyr(s))
   - Cat and Mouse Act attracted sympathy
   - media attention
   - Suffragettes gave up militancy on outbreak of war
   - effect of women's war work

Unit II—Context A: 1790s–1820s

Section A

1. (a) The candidate assesses the importance of the fear of revolution in causing war between France and other European powers using **evidence** such as:
   - leading European powers were opposed to revolutionary ideas (liberty, equality)

1. (a) (continued)
- European rulers supported the French King against his opponents
- French Queen was of the Austrian royal family
- French exiles fled to other countries and spread anti-revolutionary ideas
- French troops were believed to carry revolutionary ideas wherever they went
- execution of French King (and Queen) turned many against revolution
- Edict of Fraternity encouraged people to revolution
- Reign of Terror was too extreme; led to growing opposition
- popular unrest, supporting French Revolution, broke out in some countries

(b) The candidate assesses the importance of aggressive French foreign policy in causing war using **evidence** such as:
- Louis XVI's ministers (both Girondins and Monarchists) favoured the idea of war (for different reasons)
- April 1792 – France declared war on Austria and Prussia
- Edict of Fraternity was equivalent to a declaration of war against European monarchies
- French actions showed contempt for British neutrality
- France sent an army into Austrian Netherlands
- France declared River Scheldt open to international navigation: in violation of various treaties
- Britain was alarmed at French incursions into Low Countries (against British foreign policy)
- French actions threatened Britain's commercial importance
- French actions threatened Britain's naval supremacy
- France threatened to (and later did) invade Holland
- French actions upset European balance of power
- March 1793 – France declared war on Britain, Holland and then Spain
- August 1793 – First Coalition formed against fear of French actions

Other factors contributing to outbreak of war.

Section B

2. The candidate discusses the attitude of the author of Source A using **evidence** such as:
   - author supports French Revolution
   - recognises widespread interest in events in France
   - believes that some violence is inevitable
   - surprised there had not been more violence
   - thinks French example has kindled a flame of support (for further revolution)
   - hopes others will follow French example
   - hopes it brings about downfall of undemocratic rulers

3. The candidate evaluates the fullness of the reaction to the French Revolution given in Sources A and B using **presented evidence** such as:
   - initial widespread support
   - support in both Scotland and England
   - desire for similar changes elsewhere

3. (continued)
- initial toleration of some violence
- growing violence led to a change of attitude
- French aggression turned some opinion against Revolution
- ruling class in Britain turned against Revolution

and from **recalled evidence** such as:
- some opposed Revolution from the start
- Edmund Burke's "Reflections" was hostile
- some writers like Thomas Paine championed the Revolution
- reform societies grew
- popular demonstrations for the Revolution were held
- in Scotland: attitude of people like Robert Burns
- attitude of Thomas Muir and "Friends of the People"
- growing fear that revolution might spread to Britain
- after 1793 – government reaction: crushing reform
- eg suspension of Habeas Corpus

Unit II—Context B: 1890s–1920s
Section A

1. (a) The candidate fully assesses the importance of the Alliance System as a cause of World War One using evidence such as:

   Rivalries between countries as important causes of tension/ill feeling: eg
   - Austria—Hungary v Russia
   - Germany v France
   - Germany v Britain
   - Dual Alliance
   - Franco Russian Alliance
   - Entente Cordiale
   - Triple Alliance
   - Terms of the alliances/entente and the possible importance of other factors such as:
     - Pre-war incidents
     - Balkan Wars
     - Militarism
     - Arms race
     - Naval rivalry
     - Nationalism
     - Sarajevo
     - Alliance system in action in 1914

   (b) The candidate fully assesses the importance of the Naval Arms Race in causing World War One using evidence such as:
   - German Naval Laws
   - Naval rivalry/Naval race
   - Dreadnoughts
   - New naval bases
   - Kiel Canal

   and the possible importance of other factors such as:
   - Militarism/build up of armies and weapons
   - Army reforms in Europe
   - Alliance System
   - Rivalries
   - Pre-war incidents
   - Balkan Wars
   - Sarajevo and thereafter

History Credit Level—2001 (cont.)

Section B

2. The candidate discusses the attitude of the author towards gas using evidence such as:
   - it is a dreadful weapon
   - it inflicts cruelty
   - it is the tactic of a mass murderer
   - it can win ground
   - it is an object of horror
   - it is a contemptible weapon
   - it is only used by horrible, contemptible armies

3. The candidate evaluates the completeness of the description using **presented evidence** such as:
   - gas causes dreadful results
   - gas is used to try to gain ground
   - gas causes blisters and blinding
   - gas kills by suffocation/choking

   and from **recalled evidence** such as:
   - German use of gas at Ypres in 1915
   - operation of gas canisters/shells
   - types of gas used: mustard; phosgene; tear
   - operation of gas canisters/shells
   - importance of wind direction
   - use of gas masks
   - British use of gas
   - surprise factor of gas
   - effectiveness of gas

Unit II—Context C: 1930s–1960s
Section A

1. (a) The candidate fully assesses the importance of German rearmament in causing World War Two using evidence such as:
   - rearmament broke Treaty of Versailles
   - reintroduction of conscription allowed Hitler to expand size of army quickly
   - naval rearmament could threaten Britain
   - air force essential for Hitler's foreign policy aims
   - France and Britain did nothing to stop rearmament
   - League of Nations powerless to stop rearmament
   - rearmament could threaten countries in East Europe
   - Britain made a naval agreement with Germany in 1935, so accepting Hitler's actions
   - rearmament was only a prelude to Hitler's other foreign policy aims
   - rearmament was a long term cause of war.
   - other immediate causes of war
   - details of how German rearmament increased tension

   (b) The candidate fully assesses the importance of Hitler's actions against Czechoslovakia in causing the second World War using evidence such as:
   - Hitler's demands for Sudetenland—part of Czechoslovakia
   - part of Hitler's aim of a Greater Germany
   - unrest in Sudetenland among German-speaking population (Henlein)
   - Czechoslovakian response (alliances with France and Russia)
   - Chamberlain's meetings with Hitler — Berchtesgaden, Bad Godesberg

1. (b) (continued)
   - British and French attitude—appeasement of Hitler
   - Hitler increases demands—crisis deepens
   - danger of war close in late September 1938
   - Munich Conference called—Hitler gets Sudetenland
   - Hitler's assurances of peace in future ("peace in our time")
   - weakening of Czechoslovakia-Russian attitude
   - Hitler demands rest of Czechslovakia in March 1939
   - end of appeasement after extinction of Czechoslovakia
   - British and French guarantees in Eastern Europe after March 1939
   - war much nearer after failure of appeasement
   - way open for aggression v Poland
   - possible other causes of war

Section B

2. The candidate evaluates the completeness of Source A using **presented evidence** such as:
   - new Soviet missile sites on Cuba are threatening
   - missiles capable of striking cities in USA
   - missiles aimed at US capital/centre of Government
   - more missile sites being built
   - new missile sites designed to strike cities in the Western hemisphere

   and from **recalled evidence** such as:
   - secret missile sites detected by US spy planes
   - possible Soviet motives were hostile
   - Kennedy announced blockade of Cuba in retaliation
   - Kennedy announced other measures
   - US military build up
   - part of Domino Theory attitude
   - US sphere of influence threatened
   - US fear and surprise
   - threat was of nuclear attack

3. The candidate evaluates the attitude of the author using evidence such as:
   - knows that US wants security
   - wants security for Russia, too
   - says Soviet Union feels surrounded
   - annoyed at US rockets in Turkey
   - says Turkey is closer to Soviet Union than Cuba is to US
   - feels US is being hypocritical
   - all countries wanted/deserved security

Unit III—Context A: USA 1850–1880
Section A

1. The candidate describes problems faced by the native Americans using evidence such as:
   - loss of homeland as boundaries pushed west
   - loss of freedom with removal to reservations
   - destruction of way of life
   - hunting grounds disturbed
   - buffalo destroyed
   - clash of cultures
   - white settlers regarded native Americans as inferior—in need of civilising
   - decline of population: some tribes wiped out

1. (continued)
- diseases (smallpox, measles, cholera) affected tribes
- alcohol becomes a problem
- loss of power: tribes not regarded as a nation

2. The candidate explains the reasons for discontent in the South after the Civil War using evidence such as:
   - South defeated
   - Economy in ruins
   - Destruction to land and property
   - Northern troops garrisoned in Southern homes
   - Military rule imposed
   - Freedmen's Bureau
   - annoyed at rights for ex-slaves
   - ex-army personnel unable to vote
   - annoyance at carpetbaggers and scallywags
   - Blacks still have rights restricted
   - Black Codes
   - many ex-slaves worse off

Section B
3. The candidate evaluates the source using evidence such as:
   - authorship: published by Republican Party
   - contemporaneity: published at the time of the presidential election
   - purpose: to persuade Americans to vote for Lincoln (propaganda)
   - content: contains information on Lincoln's policies
   - accuracy: propaganda election manifesto poster/biased
   - limitation: only one poster about one (very important) policy

4. The candidate discusses the views in Source B using evidence such as:
   - Union will be split—a line drawn across it
   - War will be waged against slave holding states
   - South will be excluded
   - South will lose equal rights
   - South will lose power of self government
   - Federal Government will become enemy of the South

5. The candidate compares the Sources with reference to features such as:

   Sources disagree about the country being divided:
   - Source A: Lincoln says "the Union shall be preserved"
   - Source B: " a line has been drawn across the Union"

   Sources disagree about the preservation of the Union:
   - Source A: Lincoln says: "main objective is to save the Union"
   - Source B: says "the south shall be excluded".

   Sources disagree about national identity:
   - Source A shows US flag and the slogan "Rally Round the Flag"
   - Source B says the American Government is the enemy of the south.

   Sources disagree about slavery:
   - Source A says Lincoln's aim is neither to destroy nor save slavery
   - Source B says a war will be waged against slavery until it shall cease

Unit III—Context B: India 1917–1947
Section A
1. The candidate describes Indian divisions using evidence such as:
   - religious divisions between Hindus, Muslims, Sikhs etc (often encouraged by British Raj)
   - ethnic divisions—eg between northern Aryans and Southern Dravidians
   - internal differences between princely states and provinces under direct British rule
   - social divisions caused by the Hindu caste system
   - other social divisions caused by economic inequalities
   - political divisions between Congress and Muslim League: often encouraged by British Raj

2. The candidate gives reasons for the popularity of the Congress Party using evidence such as:
   - Congress policy of self-government
   - support for full independence grew from 1929 onwards
   - Congress aimed to unite all Indians against communalism/religious divisions (secular party)
   - leadership and influence of Gandhi
   - leadership and influence of Nehru
   - various civil disobedience campaigns (examples are possible)
   - gained publicity and support

Section B
3. The candidate evaluates Source A using evidence such as:
   - authorship: British cartoon
   - contemporaneity: at time of Salt March—beginning of civil disobedience campaign
   - accuracy: clearly opposed to Gandhi's tactics
   - limitation: only gives a British view (Civil Disobedience is a monster)
   - purpose: to criticise/discredit Gandhi's tactics
   - content: refers to civil disobedience tactics

4. The candidate compares the sources using evidence such as:

   Sources agree that Gandhi supported civil disobedience:
   - Source A shows Gandhi summoning the genie of civil disobedience
   - Source B states Ghandi's intention to use civil disobedience

   Sources disagree about how civil disobedience will be controlled:
   - Source A suggests that civil disobedience will get out of control (Gandhi will not be able to control it
   - Source B says civil disobedience will be "organised" and "peaceful"

   Sources disagree about the nature of civil disobedience:
   - Source A suggests that civil disobedience will lead to violence; menacing figure of the genie and "disobedient words"
   - Source B says that civil disobedience is not intended to hurt anyone

   Sources disagree about British view of civil disobedience:
   - Source A shows a hostile British view

History Credit Level—2001 (cont.)

4. (continued)
- Source B says the tactics will work to convert the British/check organised violence of government

Only Source B says that the tactics are in response to British violence

Only Source B gives reasons for the campaign

5. The candidate evaluates the attitudes shown in Source B using evidence such as:
   - does not want to harm any British
   - thinks British rule is a curse (bad for India)
   - thinks only non-violence can combat British violence
   - wants to show British people that British rule is wrong
   - plans to combat the salt tax through civil disobedience
   - feels he has no alternative to civil disobedience

Unit III—Context C: Russia 1914–1941
Section A

1. The candidate describes the hardships faced by Russian peasants using evidence such as:
   - high taxes
   - farms too small to feed a family
   - old fashioned farming methods
   - very little machinery
   - redemption debts had to be paid
   - poor housing
   - poor standard of living
   - frequent food shortages/famine
   - restricted freedom
   - further effects of the war
   - did not own land
   - oppressed by secret police
   - harsh climate
   - treatment of kulaks

2. The candidate explains why Lenin thought the time was right for revolution using evidence such as:
   - Provisional Government was unpopular
   - growing anarchy in the country
   - unrest in towns: food and fuel shortages
   - people tired of war
   - Bolsheviks promised to end the war
   - Provisional Government lost support of army
   - growing support for Bolshevik ideas
   - Bolsheviks won support through role in Kornilov Revolt
   - Red Guards now armed
   - Bolshevik slogans: Peace Bread and Land
   - Bolsheviks had gained control of Petrograd and Moscow Soviets
   - Lenin's self-belief: "Go now; Do not wait."

Section B

3. The candidate identifies the attitude of Stalin using **presented evidence** such as:
   - strongly supports agricultural change in Russia
   - believes small farms must be joined into larger farms
   - argues that workers must cooperate on larger farms

3. (continued)
   - insists changes should take place gradually
   - believes peasants should be persuaded not forced
   - insists that this is the only solution to agricultural problems

4. The candidate evaluates Source B using evidence such as:
   - authorship: official government photographer
   - contemporaneity: primary source from the period of collectivisation
   - content: shows party workers talking to peasants (farm workers)
   - accuracy: government propaganda
   - purpose: aimed at persuading peasants to carry out collectivisation
   - limitation: only shows what happened in one part of Russia/on one occasion

5. The candidate compares the sources using evidence such as:

   Sources agree that party officials went out to encourage collectivisation:
   - Source B shows people listening to a party official
   - Source C says party men sent out

   Sources agree that persuasion was used:
   - Source B shows a peaceful discussion/lecture
   - Source C talks about encouraging peasants

   Sources disagree about methods used:
   - Source B—peaceful persuasion
   - Source C—threats/violence

   Only Source B shows propaganda posters being used

   Only Source C mentions use of security men and violence

Unit III—Context D: Germany 1918–1939
Section A

1. The candidate describes the reasons for German anger over Versailles using evidence such as:
   - not based on Wilson's 14 points
   - a dictated peace
   - War Guilt Clause
   - huge reparations
   - loss of territory in Europe (examples accepted as one developed point)
   - loss of colonies
   - military restrictions/disarmament
   - ban on Anschluss
   - German perceived threat of invasion

2. The candidate gives reasons for Nazi support between 1933 and 1939 using evidence such as:
   - fear of SS/Brownshirts
   - fear of concentration camps
   - appeal of Nazi policies
   - employment increased/unemployment decreased
   - lack of effective opposition
   - Hitler's abilities as an orator
   - Nazi propaganda including radio and cinema
   - rallies and parades
   - Youth activities
   - provided strong leadership
   - appeared to solve economic problems
   - only one legal political party

2. (continued)
- strict control/totalitarian state
- control of education

Section B

3. The candidate evaluates Source A in terms of evidence such as:
   - authorship: photograph and should be reliable?
   - contemporaneity: primary source from Nazi era
   - accuracy: matches other evidence on treatment of Jewish children (textbooks)
   - content: shows children being humiliated in class
   - purpose: anti-Semitic propaganda
   - limitation: only one classroom in one part of Germany

4. The candidate compares the sources using evidence such as:

   Both Sources agree that Jewish children were humiliated:
   - Source A shows children being shamed
   - Source B says Jewish girl arrived at home after being humiliated

   Both sources agree that Jewish children were separated in class:
   - Source A shows two Jewish children at the blackboard
   - Source B says the teacher separated Aryan and non Aryan children

   Both sources agree that the Jewish children were made an example of:
   - Source A shows them standing in front of the blackboard
   - Source B says that the teacher told the Aryans to study the non Aryans for signs of Jewishness

   Both Sources highlight the role teacher played in the humiliation of the Jews:
   - Source A teacher supervising the humiliation of the Jews.
   - Source B says that the teacher organised the humiliation of the Jews

   Both Sources agree that Jews were treated as enemies:
   - Source A: blackboard slogan says "Jews are our greatest enemies".
   - Source B: Aryan and Jewish children were now enemies.

5. The candidate discusses the attitudes conveyed in the Source, using evidence such as:
   - says that Christians in Munich are against the violence
   - says much sympathy and compassion is shown towards Jews
   - says some Aryans are willing to shelter Jews
   - thinks the ban on Jews using shops is harsh
   - says grocers ignored the ban (were sympathetic to Jews)
   - says bakers ignored the ban and sold to Jews (sympathetic to Jews)
   - Christians generally in favour of Jews

History Credit Level—2002

Unit I—Context A: 1750s–1850s
Section A

1. (a) The candidate explains fully the difficulties faced by people in nineteenth-century Scotland due to problems with housing using evidence such as:
   - rapid growth of factory towns led to poor/jerry built housing
   - slum housing led to unhealthy/bad conditions
   - most could only afford a single apartment flat
   - serious overcrowding existed
   - houses built close together: back to back
   - houses in need of repair: cold, damp conditions
   - narrow closes and high buildings excluded sunlight
   - few windows reduced light and ventilation
   - smells emanated from midden boxes/cess pits
   - water supply was limited/non existent: people often dirty
   - primitive sanitation led to accumulation of sewage
   - sewage attracted vermin (flies, rats etc) and spread disease
   - common stairs and passageways were filthy and smelly
   - houses in the countryside often had earthen floors: encouraged dampness

   Further evidence in relation to problems with rural housing eg:
   - simple sleeping arrangements
   - heating, lighting and cooking

   (b) The candidate explains fully the difficulties faced by people in nineteenth-century Scotland due to problems with health using evidence such as:
   - inability to keep clean encouraged health problems
   - ignorance of causes of disease hampered good health
   - medical facilities/doctors were insufficient
   - unqualified medical help worsened the situation
   - medicines were often ineffective
   - people could not afford to pay for treatment
   - hospitals were not properly equipped
   - poor diet often led to health problems
   - overcrowding and unhygienic conditions led to health problems
   - polluted water spread disease (eg cholera)
   - poor ventilation and diet caused TB
   - rats, lice etc spread typhus and typhoid
   - people worked long hours in poor conditions and that damaged health

Section B

2. The candidate makes a balanced evaluation of **Sources A** and **B** using evidence such as:

   Source A:
   - contemporaneity: from the time of new technology being used in mills
   - authorship: from official investigation into mill conditions/based on first hand experience

History Credit Level—2002 (cont.)

2. (continued)
   - content: details of working conditions
   - accuracy: produced as part of an official report: good chance of accuracy; matches other evidence: eg ...
   - purpose: to officially investigate working conditions
   - limitation: only deals with one mill

   Source B:
   - contemporaneity: secondary source based on hindsight
   - authorship: historian who has researched the topic
   - content: good detail on bad conditions in mills
   - accuracy: agrees with other evidence: eg ...
   - purpose: to inform about conditions in mills
   - limitation: one-sided: only gives harmful effects

3. The candidate identifies evidence which supports the view that mills supplied good working conditions such as:

   Source A:
   - mills were well ventilated/had opening windows
   - machinery well fenced
   - changing rooms were provided
   - water was available
   - there was decent sanitation

   Source C:
   - new factories were roomy
   - temperature was moderate/controlled
   - new factories have good drainage

   The candidate identifies evidence which contradicts the view that mills supplied improved conditions such as:

   Source B:
   - people lost the freedom they had working at home
   - workers had to keep up with machines
   - there was harsh factory discipline/people sacked if they questioned authority
   - there were dangerous working conditions
   - no safety laws
   - no guards on machinery

   Source C:
   - old mills had no changing facilities/washing facilities
   - air was polluted with dust (no facilities to remove dust)
   - rooms were very low

4. The candidate offers a balanced conclusion to the issue using **presented evidence** such as:

   for the issue
   - mills were well ventilated
   - safer machinery
   - changing rooms were provided
   - fresh water was available
   - decent sanitation in mills

4. (continued)
   against the issue
   - workers lost independence
   - factory discipline was harsh
   - working conditions were dangerous
   - lack of ventilation
   - polluted atmosphere
   - rooms were cramped
   - no changing facilities
   - unguarded machinery
   - no safety laws

   and **recalled evidence** such as:
   - machines (Water Frames: mules) worked faster/easier than human power
   - machines were operated by water power—not human labour
   - factory wages were better than others
   - families worked together
   - children could be used to bring in money
   - work was fairly regular
   - conditions in New Lanark Mill (no under 10s/ good factory shop etc)

   BUT
   - further advantages of the Domestic System
   - examples of length of working day
   - work was tiring
   - noise of machines left many workers deaf
   - examples of accidents at work
   - few breaks: machines often kept working
   - meal times were short
   - child labour was detrimental
   - children were beaten by overseers
   - fines/punishments for breaking rules
   - workers laid off when no work

Unit I—Context B: 1830s–1930s
Section A

1. (a) The candidate gives a full explanation of why people's lives improved due to better health using evidence such as:
   - improved knowledge of disease
   - smallpox vaccinations compulsory after 1850
   - improved hospital and nursing care
   - cleaner hospitals (knowledge of antiseptics/sterilisation)
   - use of anaesthetics
   - blood transfusions (after World War One)
   - reduction of alcoholism
   - improved diet
   - better sanitation/public health
   - improvements to housing/reduction of overcrowding
   - access to clean water
   - availability of soap
   - cleaner clothing

   (b) The candidate gives a full explanation of why people's lives improved as a result of better housing using evidence such as:
   - cleaning/closing of insanitary property
   - 1855 Nuisance Removal Act
   - laying of sewers (1867 Public Health Act)
   - demolition of slums (1875 Artisans Dwelling Act)

1. (b) (continued)
- enforcement of building regulations (1897 Public Health Act)
- building of cheap rent council housing (after 1919)
- more spacious accommodation
- provision of separate kitchens
- provision of bathrooms
- provision of piped water supplies
- provision of better heating/hot water
- introduction of electricity
- provision of gardens: for recreational space; for food supply
- availability of mortgages
- growth of suburban living
- improvements to rural housing

Section B

2. The candidate makes a balanced evaluation of **Sources A** and **B** using evidence such as:

   Source A:
   - contemporaneity: secondary source based on hindsight
   - authorship: historian who has researched the topic
   - content: useful detail on technology in coal mines
   - accuracy: one historian's viewpoint/ matches other detail, eg . . .
   - purpose: to convey information on mining history
   - limitation: no discussion on uptake or success of technology

   Source B:
   - contemporaneity: written in a period when new technology was being introduced to mines
   - authorship: eye witness to working conditions
   - content: mentions dangers/technology in mines
   - accuracy: one man's viewpoint/matches other detail: eg . . .
   - purpose: to record details of a visit to a mine
   - limitation: only negative factors

3. The candidate identifies evidence in the sources to support the view that working conditions improved in coal mines such as:

   Source A:
   - steam driven fans circulated air
   - Davy Safety Lamp lessened explosions
   - strong, wire rope was used
   - steam engines used for winding gear
   - safety measures came through Acts of Parliament

   Source C:
   - common pit dangers were rarer
   - fewer lives lost
   - safety clothing
   - Government legislation resulted in improvements
   - trade unions brought about improvements

   The candidate identifies evidence in the sources to support the view that working conditions had not greatly improved in Scottish coal mines:

3. (continued)

   Source B:
   - still dangers of violent death or injury
   - winding gear may give way
   - dangers of suffocation
   - dangers of fire
   - 77 lives lost in 1865

   Source C:
   - common dangers/roof falls still present
   - cage accidents still happened
   - lives still lost
   - new machinery caused dust and lung disease
   - safety clothing introduced late on
   - Trade Unions continued to fight for improvements

4. The candidate offers a balanced conclusion to the issue of whether working conditions improved in Scottish Mines using **presented evidence** such as:
   - steam fans introduced
   - safety lamps brought in
   - safer winding gear/wire ropes
   - fewer lives lost
   - steam engines
   - dangers were rarer
   - safety clothing introduced
   - Government action brought in improvements
   - Trade Unions helped to improve conditions

   BUT
   - dangers were still present
   - lives still lost
   - suffocation/fires still happened
   - cage accidents continued
   - new machinery increased lung disease
   - late introduction of safety clothing

   and **recalled evidence** such as:

   for the issue
   - Coal Mines Acts had banned women and children underground
   - 1862 Act ensured mines had two exits
   - 1872 Act ensured mine manager passed exams
   - 1908 Act brought in 8 hour day
   - introduction of safety helmets
   - introduction of electricity for lighting and cutting
   - improved pit props
   - use of pit railroads

   against the issue
   - detail on dangers/gas
   - explosions still happened
   - flooding still occurred

Unit I—Context C: 1880s–Present Day

Section A

1. (a) The candidate explains fully why people's lives got better in twentieth-century Scotland as a result of improvements in health using evidence such as:
   - previously, poverty and medical ignorance led to disease and alcoholism
   - Liberal Reforms (1906–1914): free school meals to overcome poor diet
   - undernourishment and rickets decreased
   - free medical inspection and treatment helped protect the young from childhood diseases
   - medical insurance for low paid helped
   - 1930s: free school milk helped nourishment

History Credit Level—2002 (cont.)

1. (a) (continued)
- free health visitors helped counteract ignorance
- maternity clinics helped mothers and babies
- children became healthier
- 1940s NHS: free medical services for all
- better hospitals and dental care
- death rate fell with cures for preventable diseases: measles; whooping cough
- medical advances reduced infectious diseases: TB; vaccinations; X-Rays; antibiotics; penicillin

(b) The candidate explains fully why people's lives got better in twentieth-century Scotland as a result of improvements in housing using evidence such as:
- previously poor housing caused poor life quality and helped spread disease
- there were problems with overcrowded slums; shared toilets; dampness/bad ventilation; polluted air; poor water supplies
- post war Housing Acts (eg 1924) gave money to councils for new estates
- better houses replaced slums
- Homes fit for Heroes
- 1920s/1930s council houses were usually well built and spacious
- newer houses had bedrooms, bathrooms, and often gardens
- low rents helped solve problems
- overcrowding reduced
- 1930s growth of private housing in suburbs
- dampness and attendant disease less of a problem
- post war/1940s: Housing Acts (1946/1949) gave grants to local authorities for housing
- bomb-damaged houses replaced; prefabs built
- 1946 New Towns Act and 1947 Town and Country Planning Act limited unplanned growth and established green belts
- 1950s/1960s New Towns are built: Glenrothes; East Kilbride
- houses have modern facilities: gardens, shops, cinemas etc
- people have moved from slum areas
- cleaner environments around houses
- 1960s: boom in private housing
- 1980s: renovation of old tenements with solid, good sized rooms
- 1980s/1990s: tenants encouraged to buy and maintain council houses

Section B

2. The candidate makes a balanced evaluation of **Sources A** and **B** using evidence such as:

Source A:
- contemporaneity: secondary source based on hindsight
- authorship: expert who will have studied range of relevant evidence
- content: gives evidence of types of employment open to women in war time

2. (continued)
- accuracy: well researched but possibility of bias: one historian's viewpoint
- purpose: to describe women's wartime changes
- limitation: omits detail of other evidence: eg . . . one person's view

Source B:
- contemporaneity: from the time of First World War/women's changing roles
- authorship: reporter with first hand knowledge of events
- content: gives evidence of types of employment open to women in war time and previously done by men
- accuracy: supports evidence in **Source A**: possible newspaper exaggeration wartime propaganda/bias
- purpose: to praise women's wartime exploits
- limitation: omits detail of other evidence: eg . . .

3. The candidate identifies evidence which supports the view that the First World War greatly changed employment opportunities for women such as:

Source A:
- women had to replace men as a result of the war
- women replaced men in industry
- women worked in munitions
- women worked in engineering

Source B:
- women's work in war "one of finest chapters"
- from every class they came forward: willingness to work/all types of women
- work in nursing
- workers in town (in factories)
- workers in the countryside (on farms)
- in jobs previously done by men

Source C:
- war deaths: increased number of surplus women
- women became self supporting

The candidate identifies evidence that the First World War did not greatly change employment opportunities for women such as:

Source A:
- old belief of a separate sphere for women remained
- some still believed a women's place was in the home
- war not a turning point in emancipation of working women

Source C:
- thousands of women were dismissed after the war
- everyone assumed they would go quietly home: women expected to give up work
- tone of press changed: from heroines to parasites; women blamed for taking up men's jobs

4. The candidate offers a balanced conclusion to the issue of how greatly/how far the First World War changed employment opportunities for women using **presented evidence** such as:
- women had to replace men during the war
- new range of jobs for women
- women worked in munitions/factories/engineering
- women worked in the countryside
- war effort increased respect for women

4. (continued)
- all social classes involved
- women did men's work
- women learned to support themselves

BUT
- old ideas of "a woman's place" remained
- hostility to women's employment remained
- women asked to leave jobs after war
- women expected to go back to domestic life
- press became hostile after the war
- women blamed for taking up men's jobs

and **recalled evidence** such as:
- detail of factory work
- detail of munitions work
- farm work: Women's Land Army
- detail on nursing
- women in the Services
- examples of work in public transport
- women also began to unionise

BUT
- women usually received half to two thirds of man's wage in war time
- new technology before war had already begun to change women's employment
- girls were better educated and employment opportunities were already there
- 1919 Sex Disqualification Removal Act was supposed to open up opportunities
- discrimination against women at work remained: no work after marriage
- equal pay issues remained after the war
- women paid well during war/less after it

Unit II—Context A: 1790s–1820s
Section A

1. The candidate assesses the extent to which the fear of revolution contributed to Britain joining the war using evidence such as:
   - British authorities feared for monarchy in Britain and in Europe
   - fear of revolution/terror in Britain was a factor
   - Edict of Fraternity alarmed many
   - execution of Louis XVI (on 21.1.1793) horrified many people in Britain
   - execution made possibility of war more popular/likely
   - French conquest of Austrian Netherlands also a factor
   - French violation of Dutch neutrality contributed
   - opening of River Scheldt alarmed Britain
   - French denunciation of European treaties contributed

2. The candidate describes the hardships faced by sailors during the French wars using evidence such as:
   - wages were poor
   - wages were often in arrears
   - food was inadequate
   - ancient salt meat: hard cheese; biscuits full of weevils; lack of fresh vegetables; slimy water
   - poor medical attention
   - harsh discipline: flogging
   - detail of mutinies at Spithead and the Nore
   - press gangs
   - dangers of fighting at sea

Section B

3. The candidate evaluates the attitude of Cavour using evidence such as:
   - thinks Congress was immoral
   - thinks Congress was unjust
   - thinks Congress was unprincipled
   - says it was not based on national interests
   - feels it ignored what people wanted
   - says it ignored geographical factors
   - says it only recognised the rights of the strong (powers)

4. The candidate evaluates the degree between **Sources A** and **B** using evidence such as:

   sources agree the Congress ignored nationality
   - **Source A**: did not rely on national interests
   - **Source B**: it neglected nationality

   sources agree that the Congress ignored people's wishes
   - **Source A**: did not rely on the will of the people
   - **Source B**: people were moved about unwillingly

   sources agree that Congress ignored geography
   - **Source A**: took no account of geographical conditions
   - **Source B**: countries were moved about

   Only **Source A** says legal rules were ignored

   Only **Source A** says Congress acted in favour of the strongest

   Only **Source A** says it was immoral

   Only **Source B** says Congress showed any wisdom

   Only **Source B** says France was not victimised

Unit II—Context B: 1890s–1920s
Section A

1. The candidate gives an explanation of the importance of naval rivalry in causing tension before 1914 using evidence such as:
   - Naval Arms race
   - Kaiser's desire for a German navy
   - creation of German naval bases
   - widening of Kiel Canal
   - building of Dreadnoughts
   - British naval bases
   - Sir John Fisher's naval changes/reforms
   - construction of U Boats
   - growing naval threat

   and possible reference to other factors such as:
   - militarism
   - Europe divided into 2 armed camps
   - each armed camp was suspicious/scared of the other
   - alliance system encouraged aggression—each country could rely on friends
   - alliance system encouraged arms build up
   - war came closer as a result of tension/rivalry
   - imperialism: colonial rivalry
   - nationalism: in Balkans
   - Austria-Hungary/Serbia tensions

2. The candidate describes trench life for soldiers on the Western Front using evidence such as:
   - conditions: cold, damp, muddy
   - poor food: bully beef; Maconochie; hard tack biscuits
   - limited water supply

History Credit Level—2002 (cont.)

2. (continued)
- no proper washing facilities/latrines
- lack of hygiene: lice, vermin, rats
- health problems: blisters; trench foot; dysentery; trench fever, scabies
- barbed wire
- boredom: digging trenches; preparing sandbags; fatigues; tunnelling; bailing out
- difficult tasks: spying; stand to; wiring party
- shelling: bombardment; danger to life; noise
- enemy sniping
- coping with death/injury
- trench humour
- gas attacks

Section B

3.
The candidate evaluates the attitude of the author towards the Treaty of Versailles using evidence such as:
- highly critical of Germany's treatment
- accuses it of being based on revenge
- condemns it as unjust/unfair
- claims it is unrealistic: especially economic terms which are madness
- believes terms are pointless
- has no confidence in its success (impossibility of getting reparations)
- considers harshness to be completely obvious/apparent

4.
The candidate compares the sources using evidence such as:

sources disagree about fairness
- **Source A** says "it was very unfair/it was a peace of vengeance"
- **Source B** says it was a just treaty

sources disagree about revenge
- **Source A** says it was a peace of vengeance
- **Source B** says it is a restoration (return to the status quo)

sources disagree about the appropriateness of the treaty
- **Source A** says impossibility of (getting money)
- **Source B** says: stern but just

both sources agree to an extent about harshness
- **Source A** says it was revengeful/unfair
- **Source B** says stern/terrible terms

both sources agree about economic terms
- **Source A** says they are "mad"
- **Source B** says "terrible" terms to impose

Only **Source B** comments on territorial terms

Unit II – Context C: 1930s–1960s
Section A

1.
The candidate assesses the importance of the Czech crisis as a cause of increasing tension using evidence such as:
- Hitler wanted to unite 3 million German speaking people in Sudetenland
- Hitler denounced Czech government
- Hitler encouraged dissension in Sudetenland
- Chamberlain flew to Berchtesgaden to discuss situation with Hitler
- Chamberlain flew again to Bad Godesberg

1. (continued)
- Hitler claimed Sudetenland was last territorial demand
- Britain and France willing to appease/avoid war
- Hitler gains confidence from gaining his demands
- War preparations in the UK begin
- Hitler invades all Czechoslovakia in March 1939

and possible reference to background events causing tension eg
- rearmament
- Rhineland crisis
- Anschluss
- breaking the Treaty of Versailles

2.
The candidate describes the hardships of everyday life for civilians in World War Two using evidence such as:
- blackouts
- rationing
- evacuation
- restrictions on freedom
- direction of labour
- munitions work
- female conscription
- direction of labour
- censorship
- worry of war/casualties/men abroad
- air raids/shelters
- possibility of gas attack

Section B

3.
The candidate evaluates the attitude of Attlee as shown in **Source A** using evidence such as:
- sees Britain in a central role (at the heart of) the Commonwealth
- believes Government policy towards Commonwealth is approved of
- thinks that the best policy was one of self government
- thinks opponents (Churchill) were wrong/misguided/limited
- believes Britain benefited from his policy
- thinks that denying self government might have led to Communism

4.
The candidate compares the views of **Sources A** and **B** using evidence such as:

Sources agree that Britain thought she was still in a strong position
- **Source A**: heart of a growing Commonwealth
- **Source B**: a great imperial power

Sources agree that Britain was changing its Empire into a Commonwealth
- **Source A**: growing Commonwealth
- **Source B**: Commonwealth—once British Empire

Sources agree that former colonies were being given independence/self government
- **Source A**: give full self government
- **Source B**: giving independence to Empire

Sources agree that there were (a few) critics of government policy
- **Source A**: a limited number of people/Churchill (did not approve)
- **Source B**: a few regretted (policy)

Sources agree that some saw independence as a mistake/betrayal/act against past traditions
- **Source A**: a betrayal of our imperial heritage

4. (continued)

- **Source B**: regret as Empire had made Britain great

Sources agree that Britain was friendly with former colonies
- **Source A**: we have gained friendship
- **Source B**: tried to keep on friendly terms

Only **Source A** mentions threat of Communism

Only **Source B** mentions that power transfer was sometimes violent

Unit III—Context A: USA 1850–1880

Section A

1. The candidate explains the reasons why many Northerners were against slavery using evidence such as:
   - morally wrong
   - it was cruel and inhuman
   - did not want it to spread to new territories
   - it encouraged white people in the South to be cruel to other humans
   - encouraged bad treatment of female slaves by their owners
   - North affected by abolitionist propaganda
   - accusation of use of cheap labour—unfair competition
   - fear of international criticism

2. The candidate describes the improvements made for freed slaves using evidence such as:
   - slavery outlawed by 14th Amendment
   - freed slaves to have same rights as whites
   - any interference with new rights to be severely punished
   - Freedmen's Bureau established to help
   - Bureau built hospitals and schools
   - Bureau had the power to redistribute land
   - Bureau had power to enforce fair wages
   - Southern states grant the votes to freed slaves
   - elections to be held in the South under army supervision

Section B

3. The candidate makes a balanced evaluation of **Source A** using evidence such as:

   Source A:
   - contemporaneity: painted at the time of many settlers going west
   - authorship: by an artist who may have painted for "romantic notions"
   - content: shows wagons on the move—pulled by oxen
   - accuracy: paints a picture which shows unhampered movement; non-hostile "Indians" but does show wild terrain and oxen
   - purpose: to show that travelling west was possible/to show a glamourised view of travelling west
   - limitation: no real hardships or problems shown

4. The candidate evaluates the attitude of the native American in **Source B** towards land ownership using evidence such as:
   - land ownership exhibits greed
   - did not understand white settlers' attitudes to owning the land
   - did not understand why you had to build houses on land which would outlast occupants
   - believes that land should be shared
   - believes that land cannot belong exclusively to anyone
   - believes that land is nobody's for ever
   - believes you can no more sell land than you can the natural elements
   - exhibits confusion/non-comprehension/disbelief
   - believes that land/environment should be respected

5. The candidate evaluates the completeness of **Source C** using **presented evidence** such as:
   - desire for good farmland
   - making the American dream a reality
   - colonising the whole country with white Americans
   - bring civilisation to the wilderness

   and **recalled evidence** such as:
   - government publicity attracted settlers to move
   - gold discovered
   - ensuring that no foreign country could retake American land
   - fulfilling of Manifest Destiny
   - looking for a better way of life
   - looking for religious freedom
   - to civilise the "Indians"
   - looking for adventure
   - seeking employment
   - fulfilling requirements for further workers/professionals

Unit III—Context B: India 1917–1947

Section A

1. The candidate explains Indians discontent against the Raj using evidence such as:
   - the pampered existence of many British
   - division of society/prejudice/segregation
   - many Indians working as house servants
   - many British regarding Indians as inferior
   - British running Civil Service
   - Indian Civil Servants in inferior positions
   - British running the Indian Army
   - British in charge of law and order
   - British business men in positions of power
   - British interests in charge of railways
   - Indian natural resources being exploited
   - imposition of taxation
   - British ignoring/disparaging Indian culture/education
   - growing desire for Independence

2. The candidate describes Gandhi's tactics using evidence such as:
   - civil disobedience
   - organising strikes
   - Indian civil servants withdrew labour
   - Indian soldiers refused to serve
   - non payment of taxes to Britain
   - boycott of British goods
   - boycott of courts
   - boycott of British schools/colleges
   - return of titles, honours, medals granted by British
   - peaceful marches/demonstrations

History Credit Level—2002 (cont.)

2. (continued)
- details of Satyagraha
- non-cooperation with British authorities
- Salt March

Section B

3. The candidate makes a balanced evaluation of **Source A** using evidence such as:

   Source A:
   - contemporaneity: primary source produced at the moment of Indian Independence
   - authorship: press photograph: camera has captured the occasion
   - content: happy crowds/popularity of the Mountbattens
   - bias: newspaper photograph: possible bias
   - purpose: reveals attitudes of many Indians: happiness at independence
   - accuracy: many Indians were pleased at independence/admired Mountbatten
   - limitation: does not show all attitudes to independence

4. The candidate assesses the views of Winston Churchill using evidence such as:
   - says the massacres in India are no surprise
   - says more horrors will follow
   - says Indians lived happily together (better) under British rule
   - says British rule was tolerant (implies Indian rule is not)
   - says British rule was impartial (implies Indian rule is unfair)
   - expresses an opinion of predictability

5. The candidate assesses the completeness of **Source C** using **presented evidence** such as:
   - problems of two separate communities
   - religious divisions
   - separate education and languages
   - Muslim majorities in some areas of India (Bengal, Punjab)

   and **recalled evidence** such as:
   - Hindu majority in all India with a Muslim minority
   - uncompromising attitudes between Hindus and Muslims
   - separate electorates under British rule
   - separate newspapers
   - separate languages
   - problems of caste system
   - other minorities: Sikhs/Christians
   - Congress Party v Muslim League
   - demand for Pakistani independence
   - (legacies of) Direct Action
   - migration of communities
   - demand for partition

Unit III—Context C: Russia 1914–1941

Section A

1. The candidate gives reasons for discontent with the Tsar's government using evidence such as:
   - many Russians disliked Rasputin and his influence
   - many Russians disliked the Tsarina, seen as a German spy
   - Tsar seen by many as weak and ineffective
   - peasants were discontented because of the effects of war
   - workers discontented because of war dislocation
   - soldiers discontented because of conditions at the front
   - some angry at incompetence of government ministers
   - general effects of war on civilian population: food and fuel shortages; price inflation

2. The candidate describes the seizure of power by the Bolsheviks using evidence such as:
   - failures of Provisional Government strengthened their hand
   - support grew for Bolsheviks
   - Trotsky prepared the way through the Military Revolutionary Committee
   - key points seized in Petrograd
   - Winter Palace stormed
   - Kerensky fled
   - Lenin declared Soviet government
   - role of All Russian Congress of Soviets
   - fighting took place in Moscow and elsewhere
   - use of the Red Guard

Section B

3. The candidate evaluates the attitude of Lenin using evidence such as:
   - is opposed to/dislikes the Provisional Government
   - says the Provisional Government should not be believed
   - thinks the Provisional Government are deceiving the people
   - says the PG will not give people peace
   - believes that PG will not give people food (bread)
   - says PG will not share out the land
   - says people must fight for a social revolution
   - thinks people should not support the PG

4. The candidate makes a balanced evaluation of **Source B** using evidence such as:
   - contemporaneity: taken in 1917—at time of the Provisional Government
   - authorship: photographer who witnessed the events
   - content: gives evidence that some soldiers still supported the war in 1917
   - accuracy: unlikely to have been specially posed: records true feelings of some
   - purpose: possibly taken to show support for Provisional Government
   - limitation: only shows one demonstration; other attitudes existed

5. The candidate evaluates the completeness of the explanation given in **Source C** using **presented evidence** such as:
   - PG was not improving things
   - many workers wanted a new (soviet-based) government
   - Soviet Government was Bolshevik policy
   - workers were ready to overthrow PG

   and **recalled evidence** such as:
   - PG continued the war which was unpopular
   - PG delayed land reform which lost them peasant support
   - PG was unable to solve food shortages in the cities
   - Kornilov Affair lost PG support (Kerensky unpopular)
   - Bolsheviks gained control of Petrograd and Moscow Soviets (by autumn 1917)
   - Red Guards were a reliable fighting force—mainly under Bolshevik control
   - PG had hardly any fighting forces
   - Bolsheviks carefully planned military takeover in Petrograd
   - Lenin and Trotsky provided decisive leadership (of Bolsheviks)
   - strikes/demonstrations weakened the authority of the PG

Unit III—Context D: Germany 1918–1939
Section A

1. The candidate explains the reasons why the Weimar Government was unpopular using evidence such as:
   - blamed for losing World War One
   - associated with hated Treaty of Versailles
   - blamed for economic problems: hyperinflation
   - criticised by nationalists for giving in to foreign powers
   - seemed unable to stop outbreaks of violence
   - use of democratic government/proportional representation seemed weak
   - succession of coalition governments/lack of authority
   - weak leadership

2. The candidate describes the ways in which Hitler gained total power using evidence such as:
   - Nazi success in elections
   - use of Article 48 to govern
   - von Papen convinces Hindenburg to make Hitler Chancellor
   - Hitler becomes Chancellor in January 1933
   - Reichstag Fire
   - banning/arrest of Communists
   - Fundamental Laws suspended
   - Enabling Laws passed
   - all opposition parties banned
   - Trade Unions banned
   - Night of the Long Knives
   - Army Oath of Allegiance
   - use of propaganda
   - control of media
   - Concentration camps
   - work of Gestapo/SS

Section B

3. The candidate evaluates the attitudes shown in the source using evidence such as:
   - believes Nazi success is bad for Germany
   - says it will create a disastrous impression abroad
   - says it will damage foreign affairs
   - thinks it is a serious financial blow
   - says it poses a crisis for Germany
   - thinks that those who want Weimar to survive must unite (against the Nazis)
   - is hostile/opposed to the Nazis

4. The candidate makes a balanced evaluation of **Source B** using evidence such as:
   - contemporaneity: from the time of Nazi rise to power
   - authorship: product of Nazi propaganda/from Nazi sympathiser
   - content: shows Germans insisting Hitler is their last chance
   - accuracy: typical Nazi propaganda
   - purpose: urging Germans to vote for Hitler
   - limitation: reflects one Nazi tactic only

5. The candidate evaluates the completeness of **Source C** using **presented evidence** such as:
   - resistance "movement" had little support among working class
   - lacked large scale support
   - groups did not cooperate
   - did not inform each other what they were doing

   and **recalled evidence** such as:
   - all opposition was illegal
   - Gestapo spies
   - intimidation by the SS
   - fear of concentration camps
   - Nazis controlled mass media
   - Nazis kept tight control of the young
   - Nazi use of propaganda
   - widespread support for Nazis
   - lack of organised religious opposition

History Credit Level—2003

UNIT 1 – Context A: 1750s – 1850s
Section A

1. The candidate explains why farming improved using evidence such as:
   - run rigs replaced by enclosed fields
   - balks ploughed and utilised: less land wasted/more under cultivation
   - infield - outfield system abolished; less time wasted
   - fields surrounded by hedges/walls
   - marsh land drained
   - common/rough land farmed
   - fertilisers used to improve fertility
   - lime used to reduce acidity
   - fallow field system replaced by crop rotation
   - new crops introduced
   - better yields resulted
   - more animal fodder available
   - selective breeding of animals improved livestock
   - new technology introduced: ploughs; seed drills; threshing machines
   - steam power used later
   - long leases granted

History Credit Level—2003 (cont.)

1. (continued)
- pace of change varied
- sufficient capital became available
- profit from trade was used to encourage farming
- growing population needed fed/supply and demand
- English/Dutch agricultural examples were copied
- Scots MPs attending Westminster parliament brought back agricultural ideas
- Scots landlords invested in farming
- farming became a craze
- magazines/books/shows promoted new farming ideas
- enlightened/scientific ideas spread

2. The candidate describes the improvements to democracy made by the 1832 Reform Act in Scotland using evidence such as:
   - earlier franchise (since 1661) was cancelled
   - previous town council burgh vote was abolished
   - some of the middle classes now enfranchised/ involved in political process
   - in the burghs, men paying rates @ £10 received the vote
   - in the counties, men owning land @ £10 given the vote
   - vote extended to men renting land @ £50
   - 1 in 8 Scotsmen could now vote
   - previously, only 1 in 125 Scotsmen could vote
   - previously, only around 4200 men could vote
   - Scottish electorate increased to 65,000
   - burgh representation increased from 15 to 22
   - some non-royal burghs enfranchised for the first time
   - burgh status given to Paisley and Greenock
   - individual MPs given to Aberdeen, Dundee and Perth
   - Edinburgh and Glasgow given 2 MPs each
   - Scotland given 8 MPs – now 53 in total

Section B

3. The candidate evaluates Sources A and B using evidence such as:

   Source A:
   - <u>contemporaneity</u>:
     secondary source from reputable historians who will have studied evidence and combined their professional talents
   - <u>authorship</u>:
     historians with benefit of hindsight
   - <u>content</u>:
     details of factors contributing to falling death rate/ population increase
   - <u>accuracy</u>:
     objective, factual account
   - <u>limitation</u>:
     deals with only one factor

   Source B:
   - <u>contemporaneity</u>:
     primary source written at time of great population growth
   - <u>authorship</u>:
     official report; written by an eyewitness/a reputable minister
   - <u>content</u>:
     detail of reasons for population increase

3. (continued)
   - <u>accuracy</u>:
     based on first hand evidence: matches candidate's own knowledge
   - <u>purpose</u>:
     to explain reasons for growth of population in Dundee
   - <u>limitation</u>:
     only refers to Dundee

4. The candidate selects evidence that better medical knowledge caused population growth such as:

   Source A
   - vaccination against killer disease smallpox
   - deaths from smallpox fell dramatically
   - use of chloroform as safe anaesthetic
   - medical developments were factors in falling death rate

   Source C
   - Scottish medicine was "excellent by contemporary standards"
   - better quarantine procedures prevented reintroduction of bubonic plague

   The candidate selects evidence for other reasons for population growth such as:

   Source A
   - reasonably safe and effective anaesthetic: (implying that people continue to die during surgery)

   Source B
   - increase (in Dundee) due to growth of linen trade/employment
   - encouraged early marriages - and bigger families
   - immigration from Ireland

   Source C
   - medicine contributed little to (eliminating) epidemic diseases
   - Bubonic plague just ceased to happen
   - improved incomes (more money)
   - enhanced diet

5. The candidate offers a conclusion on the issue and shows balance in the answer using relevant evidence as presented in Question 4 and recalled evidence such as:

   for the issue
   - Lister's use of carbolic sterilisation
   - establishment of Edinburgh medical school
   - building of hospitals and improved nursing
   - better understanding of connection between dirt and disease

   against the issue
   - improved farming techniques leading to better diet
   - better fed/healthier mothers and babies
   - lowering of infant mortality and consequent increased birth rate
   - use of soap
   - use of clean, cotton clothing
   - Public Health Act empowered councils to provide clean water and better sewerage
   - decline in alcoholism
   - potato famine increased Irish immigration

UNIT I – Context B: 1830s – 1930s
Section A

1. The candidate explains why many people benefited from the coming of the railways using evidence such as:
   - allowed people to travel distances easily and quickly
   - allowed people to visit the seaside
   - seaside and railways towns expanded - creating employment
   - allowed middle classes to commute from suburbs
   - created employment for navvies and constructors
   - created employment on the railways
   - boosted iron and steel industries
   - made transport for farmers easier
   - brought fresh food into towns – improve diet
   - created a mass leisure industry: eg sporting leagues
   - delivered mail: assisting business and keeping people in touch
   - delivered newspapers, helping to make people better informed
   - cheaper than coach travel
   - allowed people to go on holiday
   - created standard/railway time

2. The candidate describes non violent methods used by women to campaign for the vote using evidence such as:
   - petitions were collected and taken to parliament
   - protest marches/rallies were held
   - speakers addressed crowds
   - letters written to newspapers
   - MPs were approached/lobbied
   - support of Labour Party sought
   - Suffragette newspaper/pamphlets written
   - campaign songs composed
   - campaign badges/flags/colours produced
   - Suffragettes chained themselves to railings
   - Suffragettes' hunger striking while in jail
   - Suffragettes called off their violent campaign at start of war
   - Women's Freedom League refused to pay taxes

Section B

3. The candidate evaluates Sources A and B using evidence such as:

   Source A:
   - <u>contemporaneity</u>:
     written during the period when health was improving
   - <u>authorship</u>:
     an official government document: from Registrar General created in 1855 to compile statistics
   - <u>content</u>:
     describes factors contributing to people living longer
   - <u>limitation</u>:
     reports on improvements well before 1930
   - <u>purpose</u>:
     to inform government on public health progress
   - <u>accuracy</u>:
     only mentions improvements

   Source B:
   - <u>contemporaneity</u>:
     secondary source based on research
   - <u>authorship</u>:
     modern historian with benefit of hindsight
   - <u>content</u>:
     describes factors relating to population growth

3. (continued)
   - <u>limitation</u>:
     only one historian's opinion
   - <u>purpose</u>
     to inform about historical improvements in health

4. The candidate identifies evidence that medical factors were a cause of population growth such as:

   Source A
   - abolition of duty of soap (ie increased hygiene)

   Source B
   - decline in serious diseases of girls/young women
   - medical inspection in schools
   - medical improvement during and after birth

   Source C
   - steady reduction of childhood diseases
   - improved medical care from medical staff

   The candidate identifies evidence that other factors were important in population growth such as:

   Source A
   - ending of the window tax (implying better ventilation in houses)
   - improvement to water supply

   Source B
   - decrease of overwork
   - decline in malnutrition

   Source C
   - cleaner water
   - better sewerage
   - improvement of the urban environment

5. The candidate reaches a balanced conclusion using evidence as presented in Question 4 and recalled evidence such as:

   For the issue:
   - treatment for cholera
   - vaccination - eg against smallpox
   - cleaner hospitals (antiseptic usage)

   For other reasons:
   - immigration to Scotland
   - improvements to housing
   - less alcoholism
   - better diet from improved farming/growth of railways

UNIT I – Context C: 1880s – Present Day
Section A

1. The candidate explains why shipbuilding in Scotland was in trouble by the 1970s using evidence such as:
   - competition from foreign shipyards
   - slow to introduce new technology
   - reputation for building expensive ships
   - poor industrial relations in shipyards
   - outdated working practices
   - demarcation disputes
   - poor management
   - ships often took too long to build/not completed on time
   - government reluctance to provide subsidies
   - Clyde too narrow to build oil tankers/container ships
   - Clyde specialised in passenger ships when people were turning to air travel

History Credit Level—2003 (cont.)

1. (continued)
- Decline of naval vessels after World Wars
- Scots yards very weather dependent

2.
The candidate describes non violent methods used by women to campaign for the vote using evidence such as:
- use of posters
- petitions were collected and taken to parliament
- protest marches/rallies were held
- speakers addressed crowds
- letters written to newspapers
- MPs were approached/lobbied
- support of Labour Party sought
- Suffragette newspaper/pamphlets written
- campaign songs composed
- campaign badges/flags/colours produced
- Suffragettes chained themselves to railings
- Suffragettes' hunger striking while in jail
- Suffragettes called off their violent campaign at start of war
- Women's Freedom League refused to pay taxes

Section B

3.
The candidate evaluates Sources A and B using evidence such as:

Source A
- <u>contemporaneity</u>:
  written during period of population increase
- <u>authorship</u>:
  an official medical report, based on facts
- <u>content</u>:
  describes medical and other factors contributing to falling death rate
- <u>limitation</u>:
  concentrates on factors relating to TB
- <u>purpose</u>:
  to report on the state of the nation's health
- <u>accuracy</u>:
  unlikely to be biased: believable Government/Health Report

Source B
- <u>contemporaneity</u>:
  secondary source with hindsight to events
- <u>authorship</u>:
  a modern historian with access to research
- <u>content</u>:
  describes various factors relating to population growth
- <u>limitation</u>:
  only one historian's opinion - others may disagree
- <u>purpose</u>:
  to inform readers about improvements in the nation's health
- <u>accuracy</u>:
  matches candidate's own stated knowledge

4.
The candidate identifies evidence that better health care was a cause of population growth such as:

Source A
- earlier diagnosis of TB through X rays
- vaccination campaigns
- fewer died from TB
- victory over fevers

4. (continued)

Source B
- immunisation has wiped out diseases
- vaccinations have overcome polio
- free medical treatment has improved health

Source C
- better nursing care
- antibiotics have reduced death rate

The candidate identifies other factors which contributed to population rise such as:

Source A
- better diet

Source B
- rising living standards

Source C
- improved living standards
- decline in heavy industries reducing diseases
- reduction in air pollution

5.
The candidate reaches a balanced conclusion using evidence as presented in Question 4 and recalled evidence such as:

For the issue:
- creation of National Health Service
- new medicines
- improved surgery
- new equipment
- better trained medical staff
- school medical checks
- National Insurance Act gave free medical care to workers
- Health visitors and child welfare clinics

For other factors:
- better housing conditions
- slums demolished
- provision of clean water
- drains and sewers provided
- increased use of soap and disinfectant/better personal hygiene
- school meals
- improved family planning
- immigration
- higher wages

UNIT II – Context A: 1790s – 1820s
Section A

1.
(a) The candidate assesses the importance of food supply problems for civilians in Britain using evidence such as:
- effects of Continental system
- food prices rising
- shortage of some food stuffs
- periods of poor harvests
- disruption to trade caused by naval blockade
- disruption to fishing
- Corn Laws

and other possible factors such as:
- unemployment
- threats to industrial production
- some business depressed

1. (a) (continued)
- results of agricultural change
- results of population shift
- press gangs
- Radicalism
- Government repression/censorship
- reaction to worker combinations
- taxation (direct and indirect)

(b) The candidate assesses the importance of food supply problems for civilians in France using evidence such as:
- effects of British blockade
- high food prices
- shortage of food

and other factors such as:
- inflation/money losing value
- production of assignats (worthless paper money)
- conscription of troops
- Reign of Terror
- wages kept low by law
- rebellions against government (eg Girondins)
- effects of the war
- threat of invasion
- growth of crime

Section B

2. The candidate makes a balanced evaluation of Source A using evidence such as:
   - <u>authorship</u>:
     George Canning, British Foreign minister: government official
   - <u>contemporaneity</u>:
     dates from the actual period of the Congress of Verona
   - <u>content</u>:
     information on British attitude to Congress powers
   - <u>accuracy</u>:
     Canning was hostile to Congress System/ state interference
   - <u>purpose</u>:
     to officially instruct British delegate at Verona
   - <u>bias</u>:
     reflects only Canning's view (although he largely dictated policy)

3. The candidate discusses the attitude of the author towards Canning with reference to evidence such as:
   - says he was (more) hostile to congresses (than Castlereagh)
   - says he was against armed intervention
   - thinks he prevented action in Spain
   - says he complained at Verona
   - says he caused a breach (break up) between Britain and other Congress members

4. The candidate compares Sources B and C using evidence such as:
   sources agree that Canning replaced Castlereagh as Foreign Secretary
   - Source B says: Castlereagh - whom he had replaced
   - Source C says: recalled after Castlereagh's death

4. (continued)
sources agree that Canning was not in favour of Congresses:
- Source B says: hostile to Congresses
- Source C says: refused to cooperate with Congress partners

sources agree that Canning was opposed to intervention in foreign states:
- Source B says: hostility to armed intervention
- Source C says: refused…to intervene in other countries

sources agree Canning disagreed with decisions at Verona:
- Source B says: Canning's complaints at Verona
- Source C says: protested about many decisions

sources disagree about Canning's success regarding intervention in Spain:
- Source B says: stopped members from taking any action in Spain
- Source C says: unable to prevent French intervention in Spain

Only Source B says he contributed to the breach between Britain and Congress

Only Source C says he reversed policy towards the Holy Alliance

UNIT II – Context B: 1890s – 1920s
Section A

1. (a) The candidate discusses the importance of food supply as a major difficulty during World War One for civilians in Britain using evidence such as:
   - food shortages
   - success of German U-boat campaign
   - rationing
   - Black Market
   - hoarding
   - queuing
   - healthy eating during war time

   and other possible factors such as:
   - efforts to produce more food
   - better diet for many
   - air raids
   - blackout
   - war shortages
   - wartime restrictions, eg DORA
   - men away at war
   - war casualties
   - some women had to nurse returning wounded soldiers
   - women had to do (often dangerous/ unpleasant) work in munitions

(b) The candidate discusses the importance of food supply as a major difficulty during World War One for civilians in Germany using evidence such as:
   - food shortages/unavailability
   - naval blockade
   - rationing
   - food queues/riots
   - ersatz provisions
   - Black Market

History Credit Level—2003 (cont.)

1. (b) (continued)

and other possible factors such as:
- air raids
- blackout
- war shortages
- men away at war
- war casualties
- wartime restrictions

Section B

2. The candidate evaluates the usefulness of Source A using evidence such as:
   - <u>contemporaneity</u>:
     written the year after the League was founded/in early years of the League of Nations
   - <u>authorship</u>:
     eyewitness: British rep for League: knowledgeable participant
   - <u>content</u>:
     reveals the attitude of limited support/confidence in the League
   - <u>accuracy</u>:
     matches other evidence that nations were not totally behind the League
   - <u>purpose</u>:
     to give British view of the League
   - <u>limitation</u>:
     only gives British attitude to the League

3. The candidate discusses the attitude of the authors of Source B using evidence such as:
   - are not too impressed
   - thinks it was negatively affected without membership of the major powers
   - believes it did achieve some success
   - thinks it was created to settle problems/disputes
   - says it acted properly over Corfu
   - thinks it had lost the initiative
   - believes that it had lost out to force (when great powers bullied small powers)

4. The candidate compares Sources B and C using evidence such as

   Sources agree that League was weakened by major power not joining
   - Source B says : handicapped by non inclusion of major power(s)
   - Source C says: serious blow was refusal of USA to join

   Sources agree that the League tackled the Corfu crisis
   - Source B says: dealt with the problem (of Corfu crisis)
   - Source C says: offered a solution to the Corfu crisis

   Sources agree that League could act correctly/ promptly and fairly
   - Source B says: did achieve a measure of success/acted promptly
   - Source C says: quickly discussed the matter/ offered a solution/had been ready to act

4. (continued)

Sources agree that League showed weakness
- Source B says: lost the initiative
- Source C says: terms of agreement altered/ powers ignored League/ acted on their own

Sources agree that League was put in place by a great power/bullied
- Source B says: great power got away with force
- Source C says: bullying had paid off

Sources disagree about fair treatment in the Corfu crisis
- Source B says: acted fairly/condemned Italy
- Source C says: agreement altered in favour of Italy/bowed to pressure from Mussolini

Only Source B says the League was created to deal with problems like Corfu

Only Source C mentions the absence of the USA

UNIT II – Context C: 1930s – 1960s
Section A

1. (a) The candidate discusses the importance of food supply as a major difficulty during World War Two for civilians in Britain using evidence such as:
   - food shortages
   - success of German U boat campaign
   - rationing
   - Black Market
   - hoarding
   - queuing
   - war recipes (Lord Woolton)
   - healthy eating during war time
   - Dig for victory campaigns helped
   - campaigns against waste helped

   and other possible factors such as:
   - air raids
   - fear of gas attacks
   - bombing of cities
   - air raid shelters
   - evacuation of children
   - blackout
   - war shortages
   - wartime restrictions
   - men away at war
   - war casualties
   - utility products were disliked

   (b) The candidate discusses the importance of food supply as a major difficulty during World War Two for civilians in Germany using evidence such as:
   - food shortages/unavailability
   - naval blockade
   - rationing
   - food queues/riots
   - ersatz provisions
   - Black Market

   and other possible factors such as:
   - air raids
   - shelter life
   - blackout
   - war shortages

1. (continued)
- men away at war
- war casualties
- families split up
- wartime restrictions
- threat from secret police

Section B

2. The candidate evaluates the usefulness of Source A using evidence such as:
   - <u>contemporaneity</u>:
     dates from beginning of the Berlin Blockade
   - <u>authorship</u>:
     official Soviet News Agency
   - <u>content</u>:
     details of the East-West tensions
   - <u>accuracy</u>:
     shows correct Russian view
   - <u>purpose</u>:
     to state the Russian attitudes
   - <u>bias</u>:
     pro-USSR standpoint, eg 'so called' airlift

3. The candidate discusses the attitude of President Truman using evidence such as:
   - says US refused to leave Berlin
   - thinks Blockade was a demonstration of firm action
   - believes Blockade was needed to assert freedom of Berliners
   - thinks airlift was a great success
   - holds the view that people of Berlin got fed and were provided with fuel
   - thinks event brought Western Europe and USA closer
   - believes Russia was testing the resolve of the West
   - thinks it was good opportunity for the US to prove its strength

4. The candidate compares Sources B and C with reference to evidence such as:

   Sources disagree about responsibility for the blockade:
   - Source B: a move by the Russians (to test US resolve)
   - Source C: planned in Washington/a self blockade

   Sources disagree about the cause of the blockade:
   - Source B: demonstration by US of its resolve/refused to be forced out/being tested
   - Source C: war-like actions by the West/a self-blockade

   Sources disagree about the success of the airlift:
   - Source B: a great success: Berliners given fuel and food
   - Source C: West Berliners freezing and starving

   Sources disagree about consequences of the Blockade
   - Source B: brought people of Western Europe closer to US/US won
   - Source C: plans came to nothing/USA forced to yield/USSR won

   Sources agree that the Blockade ended in 1949
   - Source B: Truman says in 1949: airlift has been a success
   - Source C: In 1949 the USA was forced to yield

4. (continued)
Sources agree that the situation was tense
- Source B says: freedom was threatened
- Source C says: real danger of war

UNIT III – Context A: USA 1850 - 1880
Section A

1. The candidate describes the ways in which Mormons were different using evidence such as:
   - believed God had chosen them
   - believed their mission was to build Zion – a heavenly city on earth
   - believed they should be separate from others
   - practised polygamy
   - operated as cooperatives, voting as a unit
   - established own militia/private army
   - formed secret organisation – the Danites
   - supported Indians and slaves
   - were more prosperous than many others: in farming/business
   - were allowed to create a state within a state

2. The candidate explains the reasons why the Republicans attracted support in the North using evidence such as:
   - focused opposition to slavery (while promising not to interfere where it existed)
   - were against spread of slavery
   - saw spread of slavery as a threat to 'free labour'
   - supported the Union: opposed to disunion
   - attractive economic programme
   - in favour of higher tariffs to protect manufacturing/industry
   - pledged to introduce 160 acre homesteads
   - demanded passage of the Homestead Bill
   - protested against sale of public land held by settlers
   - committed to subsidise transatlantic railroad
   - supported other transport improvements
   - Honest Abe factor – opposed to sleaze and corruption

Section B

3. The candidate discusses the opinion of the Southern senator using evidence such as:
   - doesn't consider Johnson an enemy
   - thinks Johnson exhibits wise statesmanship
   - believes Johnson's actions are noble/well-meaning
   - sees Johnson as good for the South/a benefactor
   - thinks Johnson is sympathetic to Southern needs
   - thinks Johnson deserves praise and thanks
   - thinks Johnson will be good for the South in the long term

4. The candidate assesses the completeness of the source using **presented evidence** such as:
   - anti-Black organisations were formed against them
   - Blacks were attacked (murdered, raped and whipped)
   - discrimination increased against them
   - Whites gave Blacks the worst jobs
   - armed gangs of Whites stopped Blacks voting

   and **recalled evidence** such as:
   - Ku Klux Klan set up
   - Blacks were terrorised by white hooded terrorists
   - lynchings were carried out
   - schools and churches were burned

History Credit Level—2003 (cont.)

4. (continued)
- freed slaves prevented from receiving full rights as citizens
- only a limited number of Blacks could vote
- Black Codes imposed restrictions
- Blacks could be arrested for being 'impudent' to Whites
- Blacks were not allowed to strike or leave employment
- unemployed/begging Blacks could be arrested

UNIT III – Context B: India 1917 - 1947
Section A

1. The candidate gives an account of events at Amritsar using evidence such as:
   - occurred during a campaign of peaceful protest against British rule
   - many gathered in Amritsar for a Hindu religious festival
   - had been an attack on Miss Sherwood (English missionary)
   - Governor, Michael O'Dwyer, wanted to put an end to unrest/agitation
   - General Dyer ordered a proclamation be read in parts of the city
   - proclamation forbade large assemblies
   - crowd met at Jallianwala Bagh
   - Dyer ordered his troops to fire on the crowd
   - crowd had no means of escape
   - 379 killed; over 100 wounded
   - Crawling Order

2. The candidate explains why the creation of the Simon Commission did not stop unrest using evidence such as:
   - purpose of Commission was to investigate government of India/ determine future plans
   - Commission composed of British politicians
   - no Indian representation
   - Indian leaders took this as an insult
   - demonstrations were held against Commission
   - proceedings were boycotted
   - Congress set up its own committee
   - Congressional Committee called for self-government
   - radicals wanted independence
   - Simon Commission was a misjudgement by Lord Irwin.

Section B

3. The candidate evaluates the attitude of the author of Source A using evidence such as:
   - glad that Mountbatten has come to India
   - pleased he put aside all usual conventions/customs
   - thought he was an ordinary man
   - believes he liked/was willing to meet people
   - thinks he had made a good impression/touched the Indians
   - thinks Mountbatten pleased Nehru and Gandhi
   - believes he put ceremony aside
   - thought he dealt with problems man to man

4. The candidate evaluates how completely Source B describes events which led to the granting of independence using **presented evidence** such as:
   - background desire for freedom/independence
   - India is not being created as a united country

4. (continued)
- Gandhi had an important role to play
- Nehru had an important part
- Mountbatten was involved in the creation

and **recalled evidence** such as:
- Gandhi's non violent tactics: eg Salt Tax etc
- decline of British power
- growth of opposition to British rule
- part played by Congress
- part played by Muslim League
- policies and decisions of Attlee's government
- negotiations between Mountbatten and various parties
- violence between Hindus and Muslims/partition squabbles

UNIT III – Context C: Russia 1914 - 1941
Section A

1. The candidate explains why revolution broke out using evidence such as:
   - war going badly: defeats and desertions
   - Nicholas unpopular as C-in-C: blamed for defeats
   - unpopular Tsarina left in charge: reputed to be a German spy
   - Rasputin's influence was resented
   - shortages of food and ammunition at the front
   - shortages of food and fuel in the cities
   - problems of inflation
   - Duma had little power
   - strikes and demonstrations in the cities
   - troops refused to fire on protesters
   - long-term grievances of factory workers/peasants
   - discontent with the Tsar's rule

2. The candidate describes Lenin's NEP using evidence such as:
   - peasants allowed to sell grain surplus
   - peasants had to pay a tax in grain
   - small industries returned to owners
   - Government controlled heavy industries
   - new currency introduced
   - some Communists against NEP
   - ending of food requisitioning
   - food production increased

Section B

3. The candidate discusses the attitudes of Lenin towards Stalin using evidence such as:
   - has too much power
   - may not use power wisely
   - too rude
   - not suited for post of General Secretary
   - should be removed
   - should be replaced by someone more tolerant
   - does not think highly of him

4. The candidate evaluates the completeness of the source using **presented evidence** such as:
   - many victims were loyal Communists
   - many could not understand why they were arrested/punished
   - many mistakes were made
   - many victims were ordinary people
   - many victims were not told reason for arrest

4. (continued)
- very few victims were anti communist/or wanted to replace Stalin
- victims had fallen out with authorities

and **recalled evidence** such as:
- about 10,000,000 killed (or more)
- some accused of wanting to replace Stalin with Trotsky
- Show Trials of prominent Communists held (they often confessed)
- family members of accused considered equally guilty
- many of the NKVD were purged
- many sent to labour camps - gulags
- many Red Army officers shot
- Trotsky murdered on Stalin's orders
- Purges began after the murder of Kirov
- People were tortured to confess

UNIT III – Context D: Germany 1918 - 1939
Section A

1. The candidate describes what happened during the Spartacist revolt using evidence such as:
   - Spartacists tried to seize power/stage a Communist putsch in Berlin
   - revolt happened in January 1919
   - Ebert and Social Democrats took action
   - the army attacked the Spartacists
   - Freikorps were used to crush the uprising
   - there was fighting/street barricades in Berlin
   - thousands of Spartacists were killed
   - Spartacist leaders were killed
   - Rosa Luxemburg and Karl Liebknecht were shot in cold blood

2. The candidate explains why the Reichstag fire helped the Nazis using evidence such as:
   - Nazis had already called an election prior to 27th February 1933
   - Nazis claimed fire was work of Communists/ started by Marinus van der Lubbe – a Communist
   - Nazis claimed Communists wanted to create an atmosphere of panic and terror
   - Nazis presented with tactical and propaganda opportunities
   - Hindenburg persuaded to declare a State of Emergency under Article 48
   - 4000 Communists immediately arrested; including Thalmann
   - Reichstag Fire gave Hitler a reason/excuse for repression/terror
   - helped Nazis win the election
   - gave Nazis more powers
   - Nazis could campaign freely
   - opponents were gagged; basic freedoms were removed
   - Social Democrats restricted in freedom of speech and assembly
   - over 50 opponents of the Nazis killed by S.A.
   - after election, 81 Communist deputies prevented from taking up seats in Reichstag
   - gave Nazis enough power to conduct government

Section B

3. The candidate discusses the attitude of the author of Source A using evidence such as:
   - has a mixed view about the effectiveness of Nazi education
   - children were meant to read Mein Kampf (Nazi Bible) but he did not
   - he wrote some quotations from/paid lip service to Mein Kampf
   - he didn't know much about Nazi ideology
   - he didn't learn much about anti-Semitism (hatred of Jews)
   - education designed to make children obey
   - education designed to produce obedient soldiers
   - education designed to brainwash - stop children thinking

4. The candidate evaluates the completeness of Source B using **presented evidence** such as:
   - friendship/companionship of group activities
   - role of music/song
   - uniforms
   - discipline
   - flags/insignia
   - passion/patriotism/feeling of belonging

   and **recalled evidence** such as:
   - only shows one boys'/Hitler Jugend group
   - younger boys joined Hitler Pimpfen/Deutsches Jungvolk
   - girls were involved with League of German Maidens (Bund Deutscher Madel/Madelschaft).
   - role/attraction of Hitler - the Führer
   - other youth activities: marches; parades; camping; games
   - army training/use of weapons
   - oaths of loyalty
   - element of competition

Official SQA answers to 1-84372-102-3
2001–2003